JERRY MAGU

JERRY MAGUIRE
Cameron Crowe

faber and faber

First published in 1998
by Faber and Faber Limited
3 Queen Square London WC1N 3AU

Photoset by Parker Typesetting Service, Leicester
Printed in England by Clays Ltd, St Ives plc

A CIP record for this book
is available from the British Library

ISBN 0-571-19672-1

2 4 6 8 10 9 7 5 3

CONTENTS

To Nancy

A *JERRY MAGUIRE* JOURNAL
Cameron Crowe

Tom Cruise handed me the telephone. 'Cameron Crowe?' he said. 'Stanley Kubrick.'

I took the receiver. Standing on the stage of a Los Angeles recording studio, I was now unexpectedly on the phone with the reigning recluse of international cinema, Cruise's next director. They had been conversing about details on his next movie. It was the fall of 1996, the exhausting experience of making *Jerry Maguire* was almost over.

'So,' asked Kubrick, in a flat voice from his London home, 'what's your movie about?'

The real answer would come to me days later, long after I'd mumbled to Kubrick that it was just a movie about a sports agent and his quest for meaning in a brutal world, or something like that. *Jerry Maguire* began four years earlier, in the quiet after *Singles*, a movie I had written and directed to loosely resemble an album. This time I wanted to write a movie with a real story, the kind that showed up on TV, late at night, usually in black and white. For months after *Singles* I had gorged on the great storytellers and character geniuses of cinema, stalking the video shelves and renting huge bunches of films. Anyone on a quest like this must surely career through the character-rich work of Ernst Lubitsch, Preston Sturges, Howard Hawks, James L. Brooks, Woody Allen, Truffaut, all of them hall-of-famers, but inevitably this road winds up on the doorstep of one of the greatest modern writer-director of them all, the incomparable Billy Wilder.

For weeks I watched Billy Wilder movies. There is one for almost every mood, frivolous and hysterical (*Some Like It Hot*), brutal and funny (*One-Two-Three*), achingly romantic (*Love in the Afternoon*), maudlin and great (*Lost Weekend*) – on and on the list goes. I love them all for various reasons, but the one that reached me the most was his 1960 film *The Apartment*. In the odd months after *Singles*, it spoke to me very loudly. There was something about this movie, a biting and yet touchingly hilarious portrait of the then contemporary working man and his bittersweet love affair with an elevator

I

operator . . . I can't lie to you, I just got chills even typing the name of the movie. It is my favourite film, and it was the one that inspired me to begin writing my own portrait of contemporary man, that faceless guy who puts on a suit and tie every day, *Jerry Maguire*.

After about a year of research, talking to businessmen, visiting big offices, interviewing working stiffs with briefcases, a friend showed me a picture from the *Los Angeles Times*. It was an odd photo of a sports agent and his client. Two stern-looking men in loud shirts and sunglasses. I was never much of a jock in school, in fact they'd always stolen my girlfriends and had cars when I was still riding the bus, but somehow the money-driven world of sports agenting beckoned as the backdrop for my script. Over the next few years, with the help of sports attorney Leigh Steinberg, I met and traveled with athletes and owners and sports agents of all kinds, and I began to develop the character of Jerry Maguire. The story that emerged was that of a man trapped in a cynical world who at age thirty-five, after writing an idealistic manifesto for his company, loses his power and is forced to search for real success. Throughout the story, Maguire hears the voice of the original sport agent, his mentor, a fictional character named Dicky Fox. From the earliest moment, I knew who I wanted to play the character of Dicky Fox . . . it had to be Billy Wilder.

For almost a year I attempted to meet with Mr Wilder, then eighty-nine. Wilder, who hasn't made a film in years, still lives a quietly structured life in Beverly Hills. Every day or so he walks from his home to a tiny wood-paneled office, located off a non-descript sidestreet that looks a little like the Paris of *Love in the Afternoon*. He answers a phone call or two, lunches with an old friend, and then goes home again. One day in 1995, the lucky news arrived from a cigar-smoking buddy of the master. Wilder would meet me on the following Tuesday morning at 10.30 a.m.

I arrived early, which didn't matter, because Wilder did not. I knocked on the office door, walked around the block, waited, called, knocked again. Nothing. Down the hall, someone poked their head out and looked at me. It was not an unfamiliar sight, another pale writer-type holding a manila envelope, tirelessly knocking on Wilder's door. In my manila envelope wasn't a script, however, it was a vintage poster of *The Apartment*, complete with

Sharpie for easy signage. I waited on his steps until 12.30, finally rose to leave, and it was then that I spotted Billy Wilder rounding the corner of a nearby alley, heading my way and wearing a snappy-looking beanie.

'Mr Wilder,' I said, 'I'm Cameron Crowe.'

'What have you got for me?' he asked brusquely, in his heavy Viennese accent. He looked for paperwork to sign. So much for my polished air of authority. He thought I was a messenger. I explained that we had an appointment. Wilder was then very embarrassed, almost flustered, and although he wasn't aware that he had a meeting scheduled, he invited me into his tiny office. I followed Wilder up the stairs and into the musty room that contained a few artpieces, and no artefacts from his many great movies, just a sign above the door that read, in a homage to his mentor Ernst Lubitsch: 'How would Lubitsch do it?'

The great Wilder sat in a small chair and looked at me through thick glasses. He fumbled with an old-style ink pen as I told him I was a writer-director heading into my third movie. I mentioned *The Apartment*.

'Good picture,' he said.

'My favorite,' I responded proudly.

He thought for a moment. 'Mine too.' He listened to a phone call on his answering-machine. It was a young reporter asking for Wilder to call him back with predictions for the upcoming Oscars. Dutifully, Wilder raised the ink pen to write down the number, but the young reporter glibly rattled off his number with such speed that Wilder set down the pen. 'I will not be calling you back,' he said to the reporter's recorded voice.

I gave him my poster to sign. He looked at it. 'Jack Lemmon,' he said simply, importantly. I nodded with the deepest of understanding. I felt our silence communicated much to each other. To any fan of *The Apartment*, nothing more need be said. 'We wrote it for Lemmon,' said Billy Wilder, referencing the other half of his most fruitful writing partnership, I. A. L. Diamond. 'And Shirley MacLaine,' he said wistfully. 'She was a nobody then.' He held the pen tightly, and regarded the poster. 'We had the right actors,' he said. 'It worked.'

'I can't imagine anyone else in the part but Shirley MacLaine,' I said with reverence.

3

'No,' snapped the old man. 'And I can't think of anything funny to write on your poster either.' He asked me my name again, and signed the poster carefully, dating it. It was time for me to leave.

'There is a part I want you to play in my movie,' I announced.

'I don't act,' he said quickly. 'I won't do it.'

'It's just a small part.'

'Then I *definitely* won't do it,' he fired back. In a flash, there it was, a strong reminder of the mind and the pen that had produced some of the world's greatest dialogue. Seeing daylight, I continued to pitch him on the part, and after a few minutes, Wilder shrugged. 'Let me read it. I might do it.'

I left on a cloud, and returned later to gift him with two rare cigars. He had already left for the day. I wrote a note – 'To your acting début in my movie' – and shoved the small package through the mail slot on his door. Several months later, as I completed the final script, Wilder's own agent indeed confirmed that they had discussed the acting project and Wilder was very positive about the acting job, his first ever. With Wilder as Dicky Fox, the soul of the movie was golden. *Jerry Maguire* felt blessed already. Now there was just the simple matter of casting the man who was in every scene, Jerry Maguire.

It did not take long for Tom Hanks to pass on the part of Jerry Maguire. I had written the first draft for him, but in the time it had taken me to research and finish this story about a thirty-five-year-old man at the crossroads, Hanks had written *That Thing You Do* for himself to direct, and his heart belonged to his own script. We agreed to part ways, he wished me well. I immediately sent the script to the actor who had now grown into the perfect age for the part. He responded instantly, and it felt like destiny from our first conversation.

'I like your script,' said Tom Cruise, on the phone from Europe, where he was living with his wife, Nicole Kidman, as she filmed *Portrait of a Lady*. 'I relate to this character, and . . .' He sounded surprised as he told me, 'I cried when I read it.'

We spoke for an hour, and he had read every word of *Jerry Maguire*. He discussed the arc of the character, and the minute details of the journey Maguire takes in the script. We made plans to meet in Los Angeles in several weeks. As he explained in that first conversation, he didn't make many movies and he was careful about committing to them. He was a big sports fan, he said, but it was the relationship between the characters that interested him the most. And, Cruise explained, there was something about *Jerry Maguire* that reminded him of the more character-driven movies he'd made earlier in his career, like *Risky Business* and *Rainman*. He seemed most impressed that I had taken three and a half years to write the script. (As I would find out later, Cruise is able to pack more into a month than most people do in a year. For him, three and a half years is a lifetime.) All my writer friends have long chastised me for being too methodical, too slow in turning out scripts. Suddenly I was able to wear my slowness like a badge of honor.

'Hey,' I told Cruise cooly, like I had planned it this way, 'I wanted it to be right.'

I had met Tom Cruise in the early eighties, during the filming of my first script, *Fast Times at Ridgemont High*. Cruise and Sean Penn were friends from *Taps*. After that film, Penn had joined our ensemble, and Cruise went on to his first starring part in *Risky Business*. At the time, there were several unruly parties where the two camps collided. I remember the baby-faced Cruise, unknown but still charged with obvious charisma, surrounded by his fellow actors. Excitedly, he told them of his experience making *Risky Business*. It was as if Cruise, in landing this major part, had already been accepted into Stanford, and he clearly held clues for what the future might hold for those of us who were still checking our mailboxes. In the years that followed, most of those young actors would go on to experience success, but none of them would experience it like Cruise, who would come to define global stardom in all of its hugeness.

Fifteen years later, Cruise enters the room to discuss *Jerry Maguire*. He wears razor-thin shades, and an explosive smile, which he blasts generously and often. It takes a few minutes to adjust. Most movie-goers do not wait for his films to hit the video shelves. He exists largely on the big screen, doing big things, on a large flat glowing surface. Cruise knows this, and works harder than the average person to set people at ease. He does this rather quickly, but in subsequent months I would come to recognize the

look on the faces of people meeting him for the first time. Basically it's this – *wow, he's three-dimensional.*

The three-dimensional star himself is holding my script, and he sits down quickly with producer James L. Brooks, himself a hero of mine, and me. There is a brief discussion about children. Cruise has two, Brooks has four. I have none, except for the well-thumbed script sitting in front of Cruise. But Cruise has not committed and there has been much discussion in the weeks previous to his appearance in our offices. Agents of other actors have started calling regularly, saying all kinds of things to promote their clients, from 'be realistic, you'll never get Cruise' to 'he'll never play a loser' to the words of the agent of a well-known comedic actor who said ominously, 'I'm going to ask you the question that should be burning in your heart – can Cruise be funny? And even if he says yes, he'll never audition for you. It's a big gamble. Go with a sure thing.'

Cruise opens my script. 'Look,' he says jauntily, 'who knows if I'm the right guy for this part. How about if I just read it for you?'

6

Jim Brooks and I look at each other. 'Great,' says Jim.

'Sounds good,' I say. Many actors refuse to audition as soon as they become successful, believing you must hire them on trust and belief and their body of work.

'Jerry Maguire,' begins Cruise. He started reading the voice-over that opens the movie. 'So this is the world and there are five billion people on it . . .'

The sound of his voice, quietly setting up the movie, is a powerful thing. We listen as he proceeds to read through the first few scenes of my script. There is a swagger and depth to his characterization. And more than a little vulnerability. Before long, Brooks and I are laughing. Finally he comes to a scene in which Maguire breaks up with his fiancée. It is an emotionally brutal scene, with some painful jokes thrown in along the way. Suddenly the rhythm is off, and Cruise knows it. He looks up at the concerned faces of his audience of two.

'Why don't you guys read this for me,' he says. 'Show me how you imagined it.'

He spins the script around to us. Suddenly Jim and I feel the world of actors, in all its painful tragic anxious glory. 'You want to be Avery?' I nervously ask Jim.

'No, uh, I'll be Jerry.'

'Okay, you be Jerry.'

We do the scene, poorly, but Cruise sees where we intend the laughs to hit. He spins the script back around to himself, and does the scene snappily, in a world-class version of what we had just attempted. Now all I want in the world is for Tom Cruise to be Jerry Maguire. But it will take another two months of discussion, a somewhat shaky table read with actors in New York, and continued shaping of the character so that it is truly a younger man's story. Throughout all this, Cruise's interest in the part is voracious. Back in Europe with his wife and kids, he calls regularly. He has already studied sports agents on both coasts preparing for the part he *might* do. He studies videotapes I send him of agents. He has even studied his brother-in-law, a sports agent in England. He reminds me constantly: *You spent three and a half years on this script – it has to be right.* But still he does not commit officially to the part. Finally he returns to Los Angeles, and asks to see Jim Brooks and me privately. He is late, which is out of character for the ever-punctual Cruise. He enters gravely, briefly mentioning a situation in which a family member has been heckled by the tabloid press. It is the only time I have seen him less than exuberant, and Jim and I do not look at each other as he apologizes for being late. We are sure that his dark mood is a prelude to bad news.

'Anyway,' he says abruptly, shifting gears. 'This is a very special project. I've always felt it, and I'm going to do the movie.'

And then Tom Cruise grins, famously, teeth flaring, and pumps both of our hands. My first reaction is hurray. My second, more private reaction is *oh shit*. Suddenly I feel the golden egg in my hands, and all I can envision is dropping it. *Oh shit.* I work hard to dispel this horrible image, and it soon disappears. Standing in front of me is Cruise, clapping his own hands together, rubbing them furiously, delightedly, like a kid on Christmas morning. He loves to work, and he loves to produce work, he even loves saying the *word* 'work'. He continues rubbing his hands together and grinning. And although I used to be more of a hang-loose guy before working with Cruise, this hand gesture is one that I will become very familiar with. In fact, before long, it will spread to me. The Tom Cruise rubbing-hands thing. It means, *let's rock*.

There are two other main parts in *Jerry Maguire*. One is Maguire's love interest, the twenty-six-year-old single mother/accountant Dorothy Boyd. The other is the only client who sticks with him when things go bad, the second-tier loudmouth wide-receiver Rod Tidwell. I had wanted to cast fresh-faces around Cruise in the movie. This is easier said than done. Many newcomers are not yet fully ready to step up into the spotlight, and inevitably as time runs out, many film-makers go with the tried and true.

Before Cruise committed to the part, there had been a table reading of the script. Robin Williams read the part of Maguire, as a favor to the producer, and a well-known actor had been set to read the part of Tidwell. On the morning of the reading, which was to be attended by the studio, the well-known actor cancelled, unable to leave the set of his current movie. Calls went out, agents were contacted, and at last minute, on his way back from a press conference, Cuba Gooding, Jr, known mostly for his starring part in *Boyz N the Hood*, agreed to the reading. Williams and Gooding

hadn't yet finished the script when the reading began, and together they read it aloud for the first time. Gooding's performance as Tidwell went through the roof. Robin Williams had reached over the table and hugged Cuba emotionally at the end of the reading.

'I hope you give me the part,' Gooding told me at the time. 'You do what you have to do, but I want this part.'

Months later, Cruise was in town and he was now our Jerry Maguire. I'll be honest. As electric as Cuba was in the part that day, there were other actors I had planned to audition too. The character as written was much taller than Gooding, who is of taller-than-average height. Somehow, I felt I needed someone very tall. I auditioned tall actors of all types, including athletes. Several had even read with Cruise, and while there were contenders, Cuba stayed the front-runner. It was time for Cuba to meet Cruise. I called Gooding Jr at his home one night to ask him to an audition with Tom the next day. Cuba's wife Sarah quietly told me the actor was home, and went to get him in the next room. After a moment, I heard shouting and yelling. His voice was getting closer. Finally the phone rose to his mouth. '*Here I come*,' he was bellowing happily. '*Here I come!*' He had been waiting for this call for weeks, working out, adding muscle tone, waiting for his next shot at the part. 'Whenever you want me, I'll be there . . . I'm going to *do it for you*.' His voice was echoing off the walls of his home. I told him about reading with Cruise, and how I needed him to bring all his fire to the audition.

'*Don't worry about me*,' Cuba shouted. 'I'm gonna *pee all over this part*.'

Telling Cruise this story the next morning, he began rubbing his hands together and laughing. Already I had found Cruise to be a true connoisseur of the work ethic, and Cuba's enthusiasm was of a rare vintage. Cruise, who had worked briefly with Cuba in *A Few Good Men*, could barely wait to act with this fellow actor who couldn't wait to act with him. Later that morning, the door busted open to the office, and in walked Cuba, ready to rumble, shouting, '*Let's do it . . . Let's read this motherfucker*!!!'

He shook hands with Cruise. '*Let's do it*!!' he told Tom.

I announced that we would read the Locker Room scene. In the scene, a bitter Rod Tidwell has just emerged from the shower, dripping wet, to browbeat his agent over the disappointing details of a contract negotiation.

'Am I naked in this scene?' asked Cuba.

'Yes.'

Cuba snapped down his pants, and stood naked. 'Come on, let's go,' he said. Stunned and laughing, we watched as Cuba beckoned with his hands, as in *bring it on*. 'Come on, let's read the scene,' he shouted, joyously. 'I'm gonna get this part. I ain't afraid of *nothing*. I'm gonna *knock this motherfucker out of the park*.'

Within a week he had the part of Rod Tidwell. A quick rewrite turned the character into a player who some felt was 'too short for the NFL'. In the end, it helped add to the plight of the character.

I called some of the contenders to thank them, and tell them I was giving the part to Cuba Gooding. By the time I called Gooding himself to tell him he had the part, he already knew. 'They all called me already,' he said, 'I said, "What are you so mad about? I watched you get all those other parts. Now it's my turn."' He was quite moved he had actually gotten the part. Quietly, he added, 'There aren't that many big parts for a black actor in Hollywood. We all know everything.'

I knew then what I had suspected earlier. The bravado, the shouting, the controlled mayhem, the pants incident, it was all part of his dead-on interpretation of the character, Rod Tidwell. The serious and thoughtful man on the phone was now Cuba Gooding, Jr. 'This is my shot,' he told me. 'This is my shot.'

'She is not quite right for the part,' said the casting director, Gail Levin, 'but I wanted you to meet Renee Zellweger.'

Well, she wasn't that *wrong* for the part. In walked Zellweger, twenty-six, a veteran of several smaller independent movies, then fresh off her first dramatic role in Dan Ireland's *Whole Wide World*. Wearing no make-up, ripped Levi's and cowboy boots, her Texas twang in full bloom, Renee came loping into the room. It was Christmas season, 1995, and she was full of stories about her dog, Woof. She was an odd combination of goofy and ethereal, and her laugh was uncomfortably loud, but her audition as Dorothy Boyd had the ring of a real person. We were clearly a long way from Hollywood, a good place to be with a character meant to melt the professional steel of Jerry Maguire. I gave a call to Jim Brooks later

11

that night, and told him about Renee. 'I'm not sure she's right for the part, but somebody's going to get a great performance out of her. She's definitely going to be a star.' Suddenly Renee fever was in the air. Gail Levin called Renee back in to read again the next day, this time with producer Brooks in the room.

The next day, Renee returned in a much different state. Her dog had been sick, she was rattled, the spark of the previous day was missing and the scenes suddenly felt different. Suddenly the depth of the character was missing. Her words felt soggy, like the brown jacket that hung off Zellweger's now stooped shoulders. It was one of those moments that is never discussed in those fizzy interviews where actors discuss the endless joys of acting – this is when it's not working, everyone in the room knows it, and Renee knew it too. She hugged me and the casting director, surprising us both, and exited sadly as if it were the last time we'd see each other. Not much was said after she left. 'She seems too young,' I said. We discussed other actresses, and who was scheduled to come in next.

Weeks went by, many other actresses auditioned. Dorothy Boyd was the hardest character in the script, and I knew one thing from writing it, to play into the self-pity of a single mother who was also a widow would skew the whole movie towards melodrama. Honestly, I am not a fan of melodrama, especially when it's melodramatic. John Cusack once told me while making *Say Anything* that my writing is not easy to act. The key is to play it as if it is real life, said Cusack, and real life is not easy to act because real life is mostly boring. So the sparks come from the little moments, the detail, and as weeks went on, I found myself sitting through many auditions from very fine actresses, none of whom seemed to capture the effortless quirky detail of Renee's first reading.

Time was running out. Cruise came back into town from Europe, and was anxious to read with each of the handful of actresses who were in the final running for the part. While away, Cruise had been pouring over each of the scenes. He carried the script in a black notebook, with multi-colored page markers for easy access. He had memorized all the scenes, already. Hungry to tear into the part, these auditions meant that the acting could now begin. As each of the actresses entered the office to meet Cruise, I watched them move through the same mental journey that I had traveled weeks before. To many, Cruise has become defined by the hugeness of his success. But the man they meet in the room is not a corporation, not McDonald's or Magnavox. Surprisingly, he is a super-amped fellow actor with a black notebook who has seen much of their work and is anxious to mix it up with his peers. Within a few minutes, the glossy expectations would drift out the window and I could see the delight in the young actors working with him. And it was returned double-fold by Cruise, who in recent years had found himself largely paired with the older greats of Hollywood. 'Great to meet you,' the younger actors would tell Cruise as they left the room, 'I mean, *really*.'

Day by day, layer by layer, Cruise began to strip down to the part that many had told me he would never do – a lovable, lost loser. As he mentioned to me one day, 'I have a piece of paper near the mirror, and I see it every day. It says "Relax." If I can relax, I can be loose, and if I'm loose . . . I can go places I've never been before as an actor. Any time you want, just tell me to relax. It'll help me.' It was a pact I made with him on the spot. In the course of making *Jerry Maguire*, I would only have to tell him to relax a couple of times. Each time he thanked me profusely, and generally tried something wild and loony in the next take. Those takes are not in the movie, but the *next* ones are. Cruise's process of deconstructing was entertaining to watch. If the scene required him to be out of breath, he would jump rope furiously just before a take, and then quickly say 'Let's go.' If the take required him to cry, he would take as long as necessary, sitting alone, sometimes listening to music on a Walkman, reaching into places that clearly wrenched him to visit. He would look over to me, and nod, and I would say 'Action.' The scene would begin. As in the final scene of the movie between Dorothy Boyd and Jerry Maguire, the level of his personal commitment to the part was constantly surprising to me as a director. As a writer, I was often floored.

'Wow,' I said, after he performed the take that is now his final close-up in the movie. I was wiping silly tears from my eyes.

'Your words, man,' he said. 'You spent three and a half years on this script.'

But this was all to come. It was now January, filming was

scheduled to begin in March, and still we had no Dorothy Boyd. One of the scenes we tried with each actress was one in which Jerry Maguire comes over to Dorothy Boyd's apartment. He is drunk in the scene, he has lost nearly everything, and is struggling with his new image of loser. The long scene ends with him putting on sunglasses and declaring with dark irony: 'Hey, I'm back.' With each actress, Cruise got looser and looser. And leaving on that note of false bravado, stumbling out the door, sometimes banging his head on the way, the room is then empty save for the actress who has just acted with him. With the exception of only one, eight actresses turned to me and said the same thing, as if they had just seen Al Gore do a line of tequila shots. 'Wow. He's *funny*.'

Perhaps it was not fair to many of these skilled actresses. What I was looking for in the character was something very specific. Once again, the road led me back to Billy Wilder and *The Apartment*. I was looking for the young Shirley MacLaine, or more accurately, I was looking for the Fran Kubelick, the spunky, looking-life-in-the-eye-without-self-pity character she played opposite Jack Lemmon. It was coming down to the wire, and each auditioning actress provided a glimpse of a different movie. The decision was a huge one, and at the end of a long day of auditions, I was surprised to hear the return of a familiar name.

'I invited Renee Zellweger back,' said Gail Levin. 'Just because you liked her so much on her first audition.'

Levin went to get Renee and instinctively, even though I was leaning toward another actress, I grabbed a small video camera stashed in my bag. Whatever happened, I thought it would make a culturally interesting piece of video. Indie-film Renee meeting *Mission Impossible* Cruise for the first time, and all that. True to form, Zellweger launched into the room like a torpedo gone haywire. She had nothing to lose, or so it seemed, and I watched through the lens of my video camera as, arms folded, a bemused Cruise regarded this Texas tornado ripping through our office. It's a funny frame, and one that I later printed off a TV screen and kept in my notebook. Zellweger read a few scenes with Tom, and each sentence of these now familiar scenes sounded fresh again. The differences between the two actors made for palpable chemistry, sexual and emotional. Then, just as she'd entered, Renee ricocheted back out of the room, but this time she left a silence of a different kind. There was nothing predictable about this woman. She cried when she should have been laughing, and she laughed when she should have been crying.

'There's your Shirley MacLaine,' said Jim Brooks.

Silently, grinning, Tom Cruise began to rub his hands together furiously. *Let's rock*.

Rehearsals for *Jerry Maguire* began at the end of February. Cruise entered on time every day, excruciatingly punctual, which I am sadly not, and he arrived blazingly prepared, which I luckily am. Preparation is a big deal to him. This is part of his process. He knows all of his lines, and everybody else's too. I used to think that, true to legend, James Brown was probably the hardest working man in show business. Today, I wonder. James Brown almost certainly sleeps, and while he is sleeping, you can bet that Tom Cruise is still up, preparing for tomorrow. I was late on the second day of rehearsals. Cruise was already there, of course.

'Tom Cruise,' he said, extending his hand. 'Let's work.'

It had come time to schedule the movie. I told assistant director Jerry Ziesmer that for good luck, I would like my first shot to be Billy Wilder's scene as Dicky Fox. Cruise and I had spent many a moment congratulating ourselves on this casting coup. I couldn't wait to film it. I began calling Mr Wilder, leaving messages, leaving my number carefully and slowly. He did not return the calls. I called Wilder's agent, and was informed that Wilder had decided against the part. He suggested that I call Wilder's number. Perhaps I would get lucky, and he would pick up the phone. Days passed, and Wilder did not answer the phone. As rehearsals continued, I collared a production assistant, gave him the address of Wilder's office and told him to stake out the office and report in when Wilder arrived.

The next day, the PA called to say Wilder had entered his office. I dialed the number, and Wilder picked up the phone with a grunt. 'Hallo.'

'Mr Wilder, this is Cameron Crowe. Perhaps you remember me from a few months back. I'm making a movie called *Jerry Maguire* with Tom Cruise and . . .'

'No,' he said. 'I'm not an actor.'

'It's a small but important part and –'

'Why are you doing this to me? I said no. I'm too old for this. Leave me alone.'

The great man hung up on me.

Stoop-shouldered I re-entered the rehearsal room. Bonnie Hunt, who had been cast as Laurel, Dorothy's protective sister, asked me what was wrong. As Cruise neared, I explained what happened. Cruise listened carefully. Bonnie Hunt had rearranged a complicated schedule to be in town for this rehearsal, but she didn't miss a beat.

'Get in the car,' she said, 'go to his office and talk to him.'

'I'll go with you,' said Cruise.

'Let's go,' I said. I felt like Jack Lord in *Hawaii Five-O*.

We screamed through the rainy streets, into Beverly Hills, and pulled up to Wilder's small office. The PA stationed outside was still there. 'He hasn't left yet.' We had organized this venture with the surgical precision of a swat team. Cruise and I bounded up the steps, filled with purpose, and I knocked on the unmarked wooden door to the office. After a few beats, the door swung open. Wilder stood there, dapper as always, blinking behind his glasses.

'I called you earlier,' I said. 'Tom Cruise and I wanted to discuss our movie with you in person.'

The greatest living writer-director looked at me, and then looked at Cruise. 'Well, I guess I can't throw you out,' he muttered. He turned and beckoned us inside. We sat on two small wooden chairs, like two earnest schoolboys. 'You won't change my mind, but go ahead.'

I went first, explaining that it would only take a single day. A single shot. In fact, we could film it in his office. I mentioned *The Apartment*, and how I had been lucky enough to find the perfect actor, Cruise, and now I couldn't settle for less than the perfect Dicky Fox.

'What is the story of your movie?' he said.

I began to tell Billy Wilder the story of my movie. It was about a sports agent, who writes a twenty-five page Mission Statement, a suggestion for the future of his company, and this one brief moment of honorability becomes the beginning of his undoing. Wilder himself listened to the Wilderesque set-up of my movie. He had only one comment.

17

'And why do we care about this sports agent to begin with?' he said simply.

I took a breath, and looked over at Cruise, who was listening intently. *Great*, I thought. Three and a half years writing the script, and it takes the now ninety-year-old Billy Wilder two minutes to dismantle the whole fucking thing. I began to explain the first few scenes of the movie, how a kid tells Maguire he is shallow, and it strikes at the very heart of who he is . . . Wilder is not buying it and now I could notice Cruise fidgeting nervously too. I began talking about Dicky Fox, Maguire's mentor, who was the voice of reason throughout the movie.

'Hire an actor,' said Wilder, firmly, ending my rambling pitch. 'You must always hire an *actor*. Even if it's a cab driver in a scene where the cab driver says *nothing*, hire an actor. I am not an actor. I will just fuck up your movie.'

Then Cruise leaned forward, and took his shot. It was a sight to behold. Directly and passionately, he began speaking to Wilder about the performance that was so important to both of us. Suddenly the chemistry of the room shifted, and Wilder knew it. He snapped back to attention. The cloudiness in his eyes disappeared. Tom Cruise was clearly the man for this sales job. Earnestly, the globe's best known male actor explained that it was a simple shot, spoken directly to the camera. It was not so much an acting job as a documentary-style appearance. And it would be done within an hour. The room was suddenly filled with hope. From the small wired window behind Wilder, sunlight fell on his cluttered desk. In another moment, I would volunteer to do the part, and I cannot act. Wilder stared at Cruise thoughtfully for a long moment.

'No,' said Wilder. 'I am too old to be in front of the camera.' His answer felt definitive, but he clearly enjoyed it more when Cruise asked.

And then, in classic Wilder form, he asked Cruise, who was wearing black jeans and a dress shirt, if this was how he dresses in public. Cruise said yes. Wilder then explained that in his day, stars dressed up, even if they were going to the grocery store. This is what the fans want, said Wilder. Cruise looked wounded, staring down at his shirt. It occurred to me that I would never be in this office again.

18

'Mr Wilder,' I blurted, 'I want to tell you this. You know that sign above your door, "What would Lubitsch do?" Here's what I think when I'm writing. "What would Wilder do?" And Wilder would put Wilder in this movie.'

Wilder looked at me like I was either speaking Zulu, or had just broken the world's record for brown-nosing. 'Is this your first picture,' he asked me.

'Third.'

'Do you ever think about giving up?'

'Yes,' I told him, quite honestly.

'It's normal,' he said. But instantly I know this was the wrong answer. I was now invisible to the great Wilder. He looked back over to Tom Cruise, as if to say 'You belong with a real director. You belong with *me*. And I *never* think about giving up.' Now animated, even showing off a little, Wilder talked with Cruise for a few more minutes, discussing *Sunset Boulevard*, Jack Lemmon and the recent remake of *Sabrina*, among other things. I realized sitting there that this profession, directing, was a lifelong pursuit and that even at age ninety, Wilder was romancing one of the world's few bankable stars with an idea toward his own future. He asked to visit the set, but dismissed the idea of acting in *Jerry Maguire* one more time. We rose to leave.

'Nice to meet you,' he said crisply, his eyes grazing my face. 'And nice to meet you,' he said to Cruise. Then, with a Wilderesque wink, he leaned forward and added to Cruise. '*Especially you.*'

We trudged down the steps, back out to the car. I shook my head as we prepared for the drive back to the studio. I tried like hell to mask my own intense disappointment. 'Okay, he turned us down,' I said, in full Pollyanna mode, 'but we argued with BillyfuckinWilder for forty-five minutes, and if you have to get turned down, at least we can tell our grandchildren about that. Talk about life experiences!' Finally I sneaked a look at Cruise, who had an odd bewildered expression on his face. It was not a hard look to identify. Not every day does Tom Cruise get turned down so definitively. Perhaps it had been years since he had heard the word 'no' so often, and so powerfully, in such a short period of time. I really hadn't hoped to be the one to remind Tom Cruise of this feeling, at least not this early in the rehearsal period. *Failure,*

the look on his face read, *I am not a big fan of failure.*

'So I guess that would be a "no",' I said.

'Yeah.' Cruise shrugged. 'And he didn't like my shirt either.'

Finally, he smiled as we splashed through the rainy streets back to rehearsals. A week later, I hired a real-life lawyer from the Sony Pictures lot. He wasn't an actor, but his performance as Dicky Fox is one of my favorites.

Every picture of me directing *Jerry Maguire* looks pretty much the same. I am holding pages from the script in my hand, and the page is mostly filled with scribbled notes about how each line could be played. Sometimes I even wrote during filming, shouting lines from behind the camera. My intense devotion to the script was matched, sometimes outdistanced, by Cruise himself, which is a good thing for a movie named after his character. From the beginning the plan was that in this movie, Cruise would be different. While making the movie, the mirror in his hair and make-up trailer was plastered with photos from each of his previous movies. The idea was to look different, to *be* different in *Jerry Maguire*. A real turning-point in his performance came early, while we were filming the scene where Maguire has been fired, and he rushes back to the office to make phone calls, attempting to win back his clients.

The scene as scripted called for him to charge down the center aisle of the huge office, as over a hundred co-workers watched, including Maguire's boss, Scully, played by Jann Wenner in his triumphant return to the big screen. After several takes we had the scene, and it was vintage Cruise, powerful and heroic, which for this movie was a problem. Then came the flicker of a new idea. Instead of moving importantly to his office, what if this hard-charging super agent tripped, and *fell* in front of all his fellow workers? Carefully I approached Cruise with the suggestion that he fall on his face. 'Let's do it,' he said immediately. I warned Janusz Kaminski, our director of photography, and we then told the Steadicam operator what we planned.

I called action. The elevator doors opened, and out came Cruise, who strode down the aisle, more powerful and heroic than ever. Suddenly, as the whole office watched, he tripped and fell on a cart. Cruise jacked forward, face-first onto the floor with a loud

thud. The reaction among a hundred-plus extras was palpable, one big fat gasp, as if they had all just seen John Wayne cry. Cruise stayed down for a long moment, the camera whirling just behind his head. I happily yelled 'cut' and finally Cruise stood. As the extras watched him dust himself off, one began to clap, then another . . . then the whole place. They were not sure they should, but they hailed him for failing. As Tom Cruise took a Chaplinesque bow, I could feel the whole movie sail into uncharted water. Some days were excruciatingly hard, other days a breeze, but rarely an hour went by when I didn't feel that I was watching a great actor take his entire super-icon persona and turn it inside out. I was on a high for days after that fall.

In terms of the pressure of making my first big-budget studio movie, I was mostly too busy to wallow in the anxiety. I often found myself relating most strongly with Renee Zellweger, whose previous movies had a combined budget of roughly half of *Jerry Maguire*. Some nights, after Cruise had rushed off to join his wife and kids, and the huge trucks were pulling out, I would sit on the steps with Renee and reflect on how we had both come to be in this position. We often discussed Cruise, the depth of his dedication, and what it meant to each of us.

Cruise approaches his work, I think, from the outside in. He tirelessly collects the details and behaviour of his character, observing and interviewing like a journalist, and then he sinks into the very heart of his portrayal. Once he is there, he asks only for quiet. Then he can stay there, for as long as it takes, with the world's most sophisticated cameras whirring one inch from his face. Even for a man with his own plane and enough fuel to fly anywhere, that very pure acting place was almost certainly his favorite place in the world to visit. Often I would say to him, 'Do you have another take in you?'

'I have a hundred more in me,' he would say. 'I'll go forever.'

Renee, the newcomer, goes to the same emotional place but without a map. Sometimes it was painful to watch her rip her chest open, time and again, to expose her wildly beating heart for the camera. The day we shot her painful break-up scene with Jerry Maguire, I was looking for a very specific performance from her. It was not easy to get, and I felt sadistic for doing so many takes. At the end of the day, I gave her the Polaroid of the exact moment when Cruise saw her for the first time, that day in our office. She laughed through her tears, and vowed to put it on her refrigerator. Later in the editing room I watched every one of her takes from the break-up scene. I defy anyone to watch these performances without getting a stomach ache. She finally did give me the specific performance I was looking for, but in the end I chose a different one. Every one of them was honest, and she experienced the heartbreak every time. I think I aged her in the process. But it is her realness that completes the once-slick agent, Jerry Maguire, and when I watched the entire movie put together for the first time on a hot summer day in July, I realized what a gift it had been that our casting director brought her back one more time, just because.

In mid-September, Tom Cruise came back to town from England, where he had started to prepare for his movie with Stanley Kubrick, *Eyes Wide Shut*. I had promised to show Cruise a rough cut of the movie, and somehow I had imagined that it would be just him watching in a screening room with music supervisor Danny Bramson, my longtime bud and fellow producer on all the movies, and the keeper of that precious thing, perspective, along with our editor, Joe Hutshing, and me. Instead, Cruise showed up in the same old razor-thin shades, bringing candy, Cokes, along with a large group of friends and family. 'Hope you don't mind,' he said, grinning, the old hands rubbing together again. Now I was truly nervous. Cruise sat in the center of the small screening room, next to his wife, and sank back in the seat, ready to be entertained. I had watched only one other movie with him before, *Trainspotting*, and the experience was interesting. Unlike many in his profession, he is not an armchair critic. He gives himself totally to the movie, like a real fan, laughing generously, experiencing the film, and I knew if I didn't hear him enjoying himself the silence would be deafening.

He began laughing almost immediately, which was a relief. I watched the back of his head as he watched and cheered on the performances of Cuba Gooding, Jr . . . Kelly Preston as Avery . . . Regina King as Marcee Tidwell . . . Jay Mohr . . . Bonnie Hunt . . . Jonathan Lipnicki as his stepson, Ray . . . and the undeniable honesty of Renee. He had been there for every shot of every scene he shared with the many newcomers we had hired to populate our movie. Cruise appeared to enjoy them all, and to a less vocal degree, even himself. When it was over, several of his family members had been crying. Cruise shook my hand enthusiastically. In the hallway outside the screening room, I stood with him for a few minutes and we discussed his performance. Across the way, I could see the editors studying our body language. I slipped them a thumbs up. For Cruise, it was all still sinking in. He commented on what the editors and I knew months earlier. The finished movie had turned out more emotional than any of us had first imagined. I attributed this to the early passion Cruise had for my script, and our pact to keep the whole movie emotionally real. The level of Tom Cruise's commitment to the part, and the level of honesty in his performance had spread to all the other actors. We decided what was then still undecided, that the movie should come out during Christmas time, which meant we would all be working around the clock to get it ready in time for December.

Across the room, Nicole Kidman talked excitedly with friends and family. I could hear her say the word 'romantic'. This was a good word to hear. When Cruise joined her a moment later, she

grabbed him and they held each other in the lobby of the studio
theatre. Clearly they root for each other, and as Nicole pulled her
husband around the corner, laughing and roughhousing, I stood
alone, feeling a great sense of completion. The feeling would last
exactly one minute. There was a huge amount of work left to be
done. Kidman and the others then happily exited for the
restaurant where Cruise would join them later. I walked back to
my office with Jerry Maguire himself. 'Thank you for this
character,' he said, still gimlet-eyed from having finally seen the
movie. 'It's the best part I've ever had. I don't ever want to stop
playing this character . . .'

At this point he asked me to give him a ride to the restaurant.
Clearly he didn't know what I am like in these situations. Showing
the movie to the actors in it is a nerve-wracking tightrope walk. I
was obviously a total mess. I could not drive myself right now,
much less transport the titular head of the international Tom
Cruise Dynasty in my 89 Crown Victoria. Cassettes were strewn
across the floor of the car. My tires were not new. My car had not
been serviced in two years. Disaster would ensue,and it would all
be my fault. No. I am in no condition to drive, and that's that.
The answer was no.

'Sure,' I said cooly.

Cruise climbed into my car, and we lurched off into a traffic
jam, full of excited and hopeful talk about the future. Just for a
moment I could glimpse my wildest dream. I'm eighty-nine and
some young schnook comes up to me with a poster from *Jerry
Maguire*.

'Good picture,' I say.

'My favorite,' adds the kid.

'Tom Cruise,' I say, importantly. And he will nod. Our silence
will say much. 'And Renee Zellweger. She was a nobody then.'
And signing the poster with sturdy precision, perhaps I will look
up and say simply, as if it had all been a breeze. 'We had the right
actors. It worked.'

Jerry Maguire

The cast and crew of *Jerry Maguire* includes:

JERRY MAGUIRE	Tom Cruise
ROD TIDWELL	Cuba Gooding Jr
DOROTHY BOYD	Renee Zellweger
AVERY BISHOP	Kelly Preston
FRANK CUSHMAN	Jerry O'Connell
BOB SUGAR	Jay Mohr
LAUREL BOYD	Bonnie Hunt
MARCEE TIDWELL	Regina King
RAY BOYD	Jonathan Lipnicki
CHAD THE NANNY	Todd Louiso

Casting	Gail Levin
Executive for Gracie Films	Bridget Johnson
Music Supervisor	Danny Bramson
Music	Nancy Wilson
Costume Designer	Betsy Heimann
Film Editor	Joe Hutshing
Production Designer	Stephen Lineweaver
Director of Photography	Janusz Kaminski
Co-Producers	Bruce S. Pustin
	John D. Schodfield
Producers	James L. Brooks
	Laurence Mark
	Richard Sakai
	Cameron Crowe
Written and Directed by	Cameron Crowe

A Tristar presentation of a Gracie Films Production

EARTH FROM SPACE

We hear the calm voice of Jerry Maguire, talking just to us. The Who: 'Magic Bus'.

> JERRY
> (*voice-over*)
> Alright, so this is the world and there are five billion people on it. When I was a kid there were three. It's hard to keep up.

AMERICA FROM SPACE

> JERRY
> (*voice-over*)
> That's better. That's America. See, America still sets the tone for the world . . .

KID ON BASKETBALL COURT

> JERRY
> (*voice-over*)
> In Indiana – Clark Hodd. Thirteen. The best point guard in the country. Puberty hasn't been easy.

Discreetly, his hand slips into his pants and scratches.

INT. LIVING ROOM

Young Girl pacing back and forth, practicing her jump from a diving board.

> JERRY
> (*voice-over*)
> Erica Sorgi. You'll see her in the next Olympics.

She 'jumps' and we –

> CUT TO:

GIRL ON A HIGH DIVE

Her actual jump. It's spectacular, as she spins in mid-air. She launches her dive into mid-air, into nothingness.

TEENAGE GIRL BOXER

Throwing punches toward the camera.

> JERRY
> (*voice-over*)
> Seattle, Washington. Dallas Malloy. Went to court to be allowed to box professionally. She's sixteen.

ON A YOUNG BASEBALL PLAYER

at bat.

> JERRY
> (*voice-over*)
> Art Stallings, Indio, California. Check out what pure joy looks like.

ON GOLDEN BOY QUARTERBACK — FRANK CUSHMAN

A line of NFL scouts watch a dazzling pass from a future star. His father, brother and girlfriend watch from the sidelines.

> JERRY
> (*voice-over*)
> In Odessa, Texas, the great Frank Cushman. Cush is twenty. Quarterback, role model, my client. He'll probably go number one in the draft this year.

A YOUNG CHAMPIONSHIP GOLFER

eyeing a long but level putt.

> JERRY
> (*voice-over*)
> There's genius everywhere, but until they turn pro, it's like popcorn in the pan. Some pop . . .

The kid misses the shot, whips his club at his coach.

. . . some don't.

HOLD ON *the kid, he's all youthful adrenalin, breathing hard.*

      SMASH CUT TO:

INT. NFL OWNERS MEETING/PALM DESERT FOUR SEASONS – DAY

A wall of new NFL merchandise. INTO FRAME *moves Jerry Maguire, thirty-five. Maguire is at home in this lobby filled with athletes and sports team owners. Herb Alpert: 'The Lonely Bull'.*

JERRY
(*voice-over*)

Now, I'm the guy you don't usually see. I'm the one behind the scenes. I'm the sports agent.

INT. NFL OWNERS' MEETING LOBBY – MINUTES LATER

Jerry sits across from an agitated General Manager.

JERRY

Easy now, we can spread these numbers over five years . . .

GENERAL MANAGER

I can't afford this.

JERRY

No one said winning was cheap.

(*voice-over*)

You know those photos where the new player holds up the team jersey and poses with the owner?

FLASH OF PHOTO

Anonymous Athlete holds up jersey, standing next to Team Owner. ZOOM IN *on someone's shirt sleeve on left of frame.*

That's me on the left.

ON ANONYMOUS NEWPORT BEACH BUILDING

>JERRY
>(*voice-over*)
Inside that building, that's where I work. Sports Management International.

INT. SMI CONFERENCE ROOM – DAY

The SMI agents are a fierce, happy bunch. They sit in a carefully appointed conference room.

>JERRY
>(*voice-over*)
Thirty-three out-of-shape agents guiding the careers of 685 of the most finely tuned athletes alive . . .

Near the end of the table sits Jerry Maguire. The word 'millions' appears often and easily in his conversation. SHOT MOVES IN.

. . . in this economy, sometimes emotions run a little high.

INT. UNDERGROUND PARKING GARAGE – HOUSTON – LATER THAT SAME DAY

An unmarked car pulls into the underground parking facility of the Houston Police Department. Chattering media members move in on the car. Back doors open, and out steps Jerry Maguire with huge offensive lineman, Bobby 'Baja' Brunard, twenty-two. He is angry, and he is handcuffed.

>WOMAN REPORTER
Was the girl sixteen or seventeen?

>MAN REPORTER
Were you aiming at anyone when you fired the shot in the Seven/Eleven?

>JERRY
>(*voice-over; curiously*)
Now, I'll be honest with you, I started noticing it a few years earlier and didn't say a word. In the quest for the big dollars, a lot of the little things were going wrong.

Jerry whips in between Baja and the taunting media.

Listen, there's no proof of anything except that this guy is a sensational athlete.

In the background, we hear Baja bellowing insults at the press.

INT. SEATTLE RED CARPET ROOM – ANOTHER DAY

Jerry now sits next to a towering white twenty-seven-year-old basketball player with a bad haircut. He is Calvin Nack. A Little Boy approaches the player with a basketball trading card.

LITTLE BOY

Are you Calvin Nack? Could you sign my card?

CALVIN NACK

I'm sorry, little fella. I can't sign that particular brand of card. I can only sign *Pro-Jam Blue Dot* cards.

The Kid looks confused. As Calvin Nack turns to grab an orange juice, Jerry smoothly dishes off a business card to the little boy.

JERRY
(*voice-over*)

Lately, it's gotten worse.

INT. HOSPITAL BEDROOM – ANOTHER NIGHT

Hockey Player Steve Remo, thirty-three, is a big man in a small bed. He is in traction, with concussion. A Doctor stands near by, shoots Jerry a look of concern. Family is near by, including his concerned wife.

DOCTOR

Do you know your name?

STEVE REMO

I uh . . . wait. Wait, here it comes. I have it.

MRS REMO
(*whisper*)

Steve Remo . . . Steve Remo . . .

STEVE REMO

My name is Steve Remo. I play for the Blackhawks.

35

(*now on a roll*)
You are my son. This pretty lady is my wife. And you are . . .
(*beat*)
. . . My agent!

JERRY
Yes!

STEVE REMO
And I gotta play this weekend, doc. If I play in 65 percent of
the games, I make my bonus.

EXT. HOSPITAL HALLWAY – CONTINUOUS ACTION – NIGHT

*Remo's fourteen-year-old son (Jessie) confronts Jerry outside the hospital
room. He's a hulking kid, all honesty, his voice still changing.*

SON
This is his fourth concussion. Shouldn't somebody get him to
stop?

As he talks, Jerry's beeper rings at his hip. He looks at it.

JERRY
(*glib, easy*)
Come on – it'd take a tank to stop your dad. It would take all
five Super Trooper VR Warriors, right?

SON
Fuck you.

The kid leaves Jerry standing in the hallway. Devastated. Music.

EXT./INT. RENTAL CAR SHUTTLE (MIAMI) – DAY/RAIN

Jerry Maguire upset in a rental shuttle. Passing through frame. Music.

JERRY
(*voice-over*)
Who had I become? Just another shark in a suit.

INT. SWIMMING POOL – *DREAM* – DAY

Jerry Maguire lifts into frame, fully-clothed in a business suit.

36

Swimming for his life, swimming toward us.

INT. MIAMI HOTEL ROOM – NIGHT/RAIN

Jerry sleeps.

> ### JERRY
> (*voice-over*)

Two nights later in Miami at our corporate conference, a
breakthrough. Breakdown? *Breakthrough.*

*Jerry's eyes open. Breathing strangely. Trembling, he holds on to the
nightstand for grounding. He gets up, takes a few gulps of air, walks to
mini-bar. Gathers some tiny ice cubes in his hand, smears them across
his face. This feeling is new to him*

> It was the oddest, most unexpected thing. I began writing
> what they call a Mission Statement for my company. You
> know – a Mission Statement – a suggestion for the future.

INT. MIAMI HOTEL ROOM – NIGHT/RAIN

*Jerry types, a pot of coffee and tray of room service near by. We watch
his face, alive now. Eyes mist. His fingers fly.*

> ### JERRY
> (*voice-over*)

What started out as one page became twenty-five. Suddenly I
was my father's son. I was remembering the simple pleasures
of this job, how I ended up here out of law school, the way a
stadium *sounds* when one of my players performs well on the
field . . . I was remembering even the words of the late Dicky
Fox, the original sports agent, who said:

SHOT OF DICKY FOX IN OFFICE

> ### DICKY FOX

The key to this job is personal relationships.

> ### JERRY
> (*voice-over; excited now*)

And suddenly it was all pretty clear. The answer was fewer clients. Caring for them, caring for ourselves, and the games, too. Starting our lives, really.

SHOT OF SENTENCE: *We must embrace what is still virginal about our own enthusiasm; we must crack open the tightly clenched fist and give back a little for the common good; we must simply be the best versions of ourselves . . . that goodness will be unbeatable and the money will appear.*

> Hey, I'll be the first to admit it. What I was writing was somewhat 'touchy-feely'.

He deletes it. And then – zip – he restores it and continues.

> I didn't care. I had lost the ability to bullshit. It was the me I'd always wanted to be.

INT. KINKO'S COPIES – NIGHT/RAIN

Jerry in T-shirt stands proudly watching copies pumped out. Wired college students, band guys, other Copy People of the Night nearby.

> ### JERRY
> (*voice-over*)

I printed it up in the middle of the night, before I could rethink it.

Kinko's copy Guy nods approvingly, taps his heart in tribute. He slides a copy across the counter for Jerry's approval.

> #### THE THINGS WE THINK AND DO NOT SAY
> The Future of Our Business

> ### KINKO'S GUY

That's how you become great, man. You hang your *balls* out there.

Jerry nods. It's three a.m., and this guy sounds and looks like a prophet. In fact, everyone in Kinko's at three a.m. does.

                              JERRY
                          (*self-effacing*)
Thanks.

ON MEMOS

being stuffed into mail slots.

INT. HOTEL ROOM – EARLY MORNING

Jerry splashes water on to his face. He looks younger, lighter.

ON TV – *Hawaii Five-O* – (*Jerry watching*).

CAMERA WHIPS *to Jerry, standing, watching as he packs. Slight
concern on his face. He moves to the phone, and dials with urgency.*

                              JERRY
Hi, it's Jerry Maguire. Uh, listen, did those manuscripts get
. . . Oh, they did . . . No no no no no, that's fine . . .

INT. HALLWAY – DAY

*Jerry walks down the hallway, looks in an open door where an agent
reads the Mission Statement.*

INT. ELEVATOR – DAY

*Jerry in suit, alone with his luggage. Dry throat. He feels clammy, holds
on to the handrail to steady himself.*

INT. LOBBY – DAY

*The lobby is filled with SMI agents. The blue Mission Statement is in
evidence everywhere. Jerry inconspicuously turns the corner, yearns to
blend in. It's impossible, the recognition ripples through the lobby.
Underling agent Bob Sugar, twenty-seven, is the first to grab Maguire
by the shoulders. ('Finally, someone said it!') Suddenly another agent
begins to clap, then reluctantly, another. Soon, the ovation rocks the
lobby. (We see Dorothy Boyd and Ray in* THREE-SHOT *with another
agent.) Jerry motions for them all to stop, but clearly he could listen
forever. It is a watershed moment in his life.*

JERRY
(*voice-over*)
I was thirty-five. I had started my life.

SWING OFF *Maguire to find two Agents standing clapping*
enthusiastically near the elevator.

AGENT #1 (BEN)
How long you give him?

AGENT #2 (RICK)
Mmmm. A week.

ON AIRPLANE WHEELS – DAY

folding up into a plane, as music and credits end.

INT. AIRPLANE/FIRST CLASS – DAY

We move past a snoring businessman, on to tired but adrenalized Jerry
Maguire. He sits in first class, working on his laptop, a pile of
newspapers and magazines near by.

The woman passenger (Bobbi Fallon) next to him, thirtyish, finishes up
a spicy phone conversation with her boyfriend.

BOBBI

Monkeyface . . . Monkeyface, listen . . . I'm not going to say
it here . . . *no* . . . Oh listen, I got you the perfect white shirt,
at this out of the way place . . . *no* . . . Quit trying to make me
say it!

*The laptop begins to beep – battery is low – so Maguire shuts it off and
prepares for sleep. Trying not to listen.* (NOTE: *JM's laptop has a
special audio sound clip when he signs off.*)

. . . how about if I do it and don't say it . . . *mmm* . . . See
you soon . . .

*She laughs seductively and hangs up. She is still buzzed from the
conversation. Jerry turns to her, surprising her.*

JERRY

Well, I have to ask.

BOBBI

(*protective*)

What –

JERRY

Where'd you find the perfect white shirt?

*She laughs, it's an infectious laugh – two strangers enjoying the good life
– as we drift back three rows, past the panel separating the cool comfort
of first class from the stuffy, airless and uncomfortable world of coach.*

*We meet Dorothy Boyd, twenty-six. A harried passenger on this bus in
the sky. Right now she is devoted to the sneezing kid in the wrinkled
white shirt sitting next to her. It is Ray, her five-year-old son. Dorothy
is covered in toys and books. Stuffed into the side pocket is Jerry's
Mission Statement. The easy laughter from three rows ahead washes
over her like cold water, as she rings again for a flight attendant. The
overworked Attendant arrives, pissed, snapping off the bell.*

DOROTHY

Look, my son is allergic to the material in these blankets –

ATTENDANT

That's all we have.

The Attendant offers a bundle of soggy cocktail napkins and is about to exit when Ray makes a gagging noise. He's about to get sick. Both women reach for an airsick bag, and get it to his mouth just in time. Their faces are now inches apart.

I'm sorry I was rude just then –

> DOROTHY
> It's okay. We're in it together now . . .

> BOBBI
> (*off-screen*)
> Don't take anything I say seriously! I love to flirt.

Dorothy, irritated, leans out into the aisle to look for the heads that belong to these voices.

BACK TO *Jerry and Bobbie.*

You're with the sports people on the plane, right?

> JERRY
> Jerry Maguire. SMI.

> BOBBI
> Bobbi Fallon. BPI. I'm producing the Coke commercials for the playoffs.

> JERRY
> Well. Good luck with that –

He politely stifles a yawn, shuts off the overhead lamp, settles into sleep. Bobbi leans into his darkness.

> BOBBI
> Can I just get a quick 'man's' opinion from you on something?

DISSOLVE TO:

INT. FIRST-CLASS SEATS – LATER

Bobbi is intense now, unburdening, as tired Jerry listens like a priest.

> BOBBI
> And I *can't say his name without laughing.* I want to eat him

up. I want to say goodbye to every bad thought I ever had about relationships. I mean, I crave this guy . . . and yet . . . why . . . *why did I have that affair this weekend?* Does that mean I'm not in love with my boyfriend?

> JERRY

I think you'll know when you see him at the gate.

> BOBBI

It's the death rattle of my singlehood, right? Because I finally see the white picket fence looming and I love it/hate it/love it/hate it/love it . . . You're right, I'll know when I see him. Why is it so easy to talk with you?! Tell me about your fiancée.

> JERRY

I uh . . . don't think we're quite at your pitch yet.

> BOBBI

Tell me, and then you can sleep.

> JERRY

She's an NFL publicist . . . amazing sense of style . . . former athlete . . . volleyball . . . world class . . . really knows how to live every moment of her life, which is why I should take a nap now . . .

BACK TO *Dorothy*

Her sleeping son now silent, she can't help but listen.

> BOBBI
> (*voice-over*)

Tell me how you proposed. I collect romantic proposal stories.

> JERRY
> (*off-screen*)

No no . . .

> DOROTHY
> (*impatient*)

Oh, tell the story.

(*off-screen*)
Oh, tell the story.

BACK TO *Jerry*

JERRY

– so our first date, she told me about her favorite place in the
world, the seven pools of Hana on the island of Maui . . .

BOBBI

Gorgeous.

JERRY

A year and a half later, we were both in Hawaii for the Pro
Bowl. Now I've always hit a wall at eighteen months. Every
serious girlfriend lasts eighteen months. It's like – ka-boom.
The curse of eighteen months.

BOBBI

That's when you need to cement, and define define define.

JERRY

Exactly. And the world does not need another thirty-five-
year-old bachelor. I knew I wanted to propose, so I took her
there.

BOBBI

To the pools?

JERRY

To the pools. Now she's Miss Rock Climber, and I'm more
the non-rock climber, but we're hiking up through the pools
and there's a fine mist in the air, and I have the ring in my
pocket, and I'm a little nervous, I'm lagging behind, and she
says to me, get this – 'Hurry up, klutz.'

BOBBI

Oh no –

JERRY

Well, it bothered me somewhat. And I got quiet. And now
she's quiet and we're both pouting a little. And I decide I'm
not going to propose. The mood is not right. Why be

44

impulsive? Now at *this* point I know *she* knows that I was going to propose and didn't. And she knows I know. So the entire sixty-mile ride back to the airport, we don't speak. And we're *both* good at that. We fly to Honolulu in silence. We check into the Pro Bowl hotel –

BOBBI

How sad –

JERRY

But wait . . .

BACK TO *Dorothy*

She is now craning out into the aisle to hear this story. It is quieter now as she listens to the easy sound of Jerry discussing his charmed life. Ray wakes up next to her.

RAY
(*waking up*)

Mama –

DOROTHY

Shhh. Mommy's eavesdropping.

He sneezes, three big ones in a row. She hands him more Kleenex, and continues listening. She's hooked on the story.

JERRY
(*off-screen*)

Now little do I know that my assistant has assumed that I've now proposed. So she has gotten the lounge band to actually play 'Here Comes the Bride' when we walk back in.

Dorothy laughs to herself. She tries to share the laugh with her son, who stares at her.

BACK TO *Jerry*

JERRY

Which they do. So, we're standing there. All the football guys are in the lobby, watching, there's even an ESPN crew. So I turn to her and sort of grandly say, 'Well, this is me, Klutz, asking you, Goddess of Rock-Climbing, to marry me.' And I

45

took out the ring, and I don't much like big scenes, but she said 'yes' right there in the lobby and some of the toughest men in football wept like babies. We're getting married in February.

> BOBBI

Jerry. You two will be together forever.

BACK TO *Dorothy*

She takes one of her son's Kleenex sheets, as an elegant flight attendant shuts the curtain to first class. Dorothy blows her nose, moved against her will.

> RAY

What's wrong, Mom?

> DOROTHY

First class is what's wrong. It used to be a better meal. Now it's a better *life*.

She pulls out the Mission Statement, and begins to read.

INT. LAX AIRPORT TERMINAL – LATE MORNING

Jerry Maguire exits the plane a few steps behind Bobbi Fallon.

> JERRY
> (*quietly, like a coach*)

You'll know when you see him. You'll know when you see him.

Bobbi scans the crowd. She spots Monkeyface, large and burly in tiger-print sweats.

> BOBBI

Oh my God, you're right. I know.
> (*as Jerry smiles*)

He's not the One. He's *not The One*.

Jerry's face falls. Bobbi Fallon moves into the embrace, faking it. Jerry moves ahead, turning back to see the doomed couple. Melancholy now, he continues forward through the crowded airport.

INT. LUGGAGE AREA – LATE MORNING

A panicked Dorothy Boyd looks through the rubber flaps of the luggage conveyor belt.

> DOROTHY

Ray! Ray!

> JERRY

Can I help –

> DOROTHY

Oh. Hi. I work in your office. I was on the junket to the conference.

> JERRY

I know who you are. You're Dorothy Boyd. You're in . . . wait . . . you're in Accounts. You have the middle cubicle toward the back with that poster of Albert Einstein morphed on to Shaquille O'Neal's body.

> DOROTHY
> *(surprised; still panicked)*

Pretty good.

> JERRY

Now what did you lose?

> DOROTHY

My son . . . My mind . . .

Over her shoulder, Maguire sees Ray rounding the corner, riding the luggage conveyor belt like Washington crossing the Delaware.

> JERRY

Well, while I go look for him, why don't you hang on to this curious gentleman behind you –

Dorothy turns, is greatly relieved to see Ray, and snatches him off the belt. She bends down into his face.

> DOROTHY

Remember 'imagination'? . . . remember what that means? Well, this is one of my bosses so you will now imagine me screaming this. Do not do that again. Ever ever *ever*.

47

She rises, shifting back to being a somewhat relaxed young woman. It's a transition she makes, oh, 500 times a day.

Well, thanks.

JERRY

Well, take care.

DOROTHY

And have fun at your bachelor party.
(*beat*)
Oh no.

JERRY

No no. I knew.

DOROTHY
(*slow sigh*)
Nnnnn. I just killed the surprise.

JERRY

No, I'm just . . . anxiously looking past it. I already had my bachelor party. It was called 'my twenties'. See you later.

DOROTHY

I loved your memo, by the way.

JERRY

Thanks . . . actually, it was just a 'Mission Statement'.

Ray has taken Jerry's free hand, and begun swinging on him.

DOROTHY

I think in this age, optimism like that . . . it's a revolutionary act.

JERRY

You think so?

DOROTHY

Oh tsht. *Yes.*

JERRY

I appreciate that, because some of that stuff . . . you know, it was two in the morning and . . .

DOROTHY

– the part about 'we should embrace what it is still virginal about our enthusiasm – and we should all force open the tightly-clenched fist of commerce, and give a little back for the greater good'. I mean, I was inspired, and I'm an *accountant*. Ray, don't spill my coffee.

Jerry looks more nervous, as Ray has now taken his mother's hand. He is now swinging on both of them.

RAY

One-two-three . . . *swing.*

DOROTHY

Hey. To respect yourself enough to say it out loud, to put yourself out there, so nakedly, so openly . . .
                    (*shakes her head*)
. . . I don't know, it got me.

Now Jerry looks concerned, as Ray continues swinging happily.

RAY

One-two-three, *swing* . . .

JERRY

Thanks. May I offer you both a ride?

DOROTHY

Oh no. I'm sure it would just make your day to drive us all the way to Manhattan Beach, taking that left down to little tiny Waterloo Street where you have to play chicken with oncoming traffic, and your life flashes before your eyes, but – hey, I've obviously had too much coffee and all – here's my sister Laurel to pick us up. Thanks, though. Bye.

JERRY
(*amused*)
Dorothy. Ray. A pleasure.

RAY

One-two . . .

Jerry lets Ray down easy. The kid is disappointed. Maguire exits to get

his bag. He then realizes something amiss and returns quickly, pulling Ray's hand up again and completing the swing.

> JERRY
> . . . three, swing.

Dorothy laughs, as her sister arrives. Laurel Boyd is thirty-six. A sturdy, no-bullshit sibling to have. The pin on Laurel's sweater catches on Dorothy's shirt as they hug.

> LAUREL
> Come on, I'm double-parked.

Dorothy gathers Ray's toys. ('You need a bath, kid.') She can't help but look back at Jerry, who catches her looking. He salutes her, with mock circumstance. He disappears, and she finds herself oddly short of breath.

> DOROTHY
> (*to herself*)
> Hmmph. Whoever snagged him must be some classy babe –

INT. AVERY'S BEDROOM – NIGHT

Avery Bishop, twenty-nine, makes love to Jerry Maguire at fever pitch. They are standing on the bed, which is in the corner.

> AVERY
> Don't ever stop *fucking* me!

> JERRY
> Sooner . . . or later . . . I'll have to stop.

> AVERY
> Oh Gawd, oh yes, it's never been better! Never *better*!!

Nearby, a large and sleepy German shepherd yawns.

> (*off-screen*)
> Never BETTER!!

The dog snaps awake, a little shaken. Avery suddenly yanks away. Breathing hard, she just looks at Jerry. Sex is a very serious business with Avery.

Open your eyes.

(*as he does*)

If you ever want me to be with another woman for you, I would do it. I'm not interested in it. There was a time, yes, it felt normal for me, but it was a phase, a college thing, like torn Levi's or law school for you . . . People change, but if you ever feel like being adventurous in that way, I would do it for you. You want anything from the kitchen? I'm going to get some fruit –

She skips off like a colt. Jerry digests what he's just been told.

JERRY

(*to the next room*)

You know. I don't think we need to do the thing where we tell each other everything!

AVERY

(*off-screen; laughing*)

Jerry, this is what intimacy is!

Jerry rubs his face, a habit that helps him process complex information.

Oh – don't forget tomorrow we have dinner with Wade Cooksey.

JERRY

I know about the bachelor party.

Avery returns. Her robo body, half-lit now in the hallway, is a glorious life-long project.

AVERY

Who told you?

JERRY

One of the accountants.

AVERY

Jerry. Your buddy Dooler worked his ass off to make you a tribute film. All those guys from the office are coming. Everybody loves you. Just calm down, relax, act surprised, and have an amazing time. And you'll never guess who narrates your bachelor movie.

INT. FANCY HOTEL SUITE – NIGHT

Jerry enters the hotel suite and overacts surprise. He falls down, clutching his heart, feigning an attack. He looks around for a bigger reaction than he actually gets.

The film – shown on big-screen TV.

It is hosted by Michael Jordan.

> MICHAEL JORDAN
> (*voice-over*)
> I have often wondered where my career would have been had Jerry Maguire been my agent. The answer – Yugoslavia.

Tepid laughs, as many of the agents turn and grab furtive looks at Maguire, who stands at the back of the room with his friend Bill Dooler. Dooler, husky, thirty, looks like a beatnik on steroids.

> DOOLER
> You hear those courtesy laughs, Jerry? There is a seething *wrongness* at the edges of this party.

> JERRY
> Oh come on –

> DOOLER
> This is fuckin' Michael Jordan, man! They should be *screaming.*

> JERRY
> (*eyeing crowd*)
> You're imagining it.

> DOOLER
> Embarrassing secrets, pointless, gratuitous nudity – this is *solid stuff.*

They are joined by unctuous agent Bob Sugar. Sugar is a Maguire wannabe. Puts an arm on Jerry's shoulder.

> SUGAR
> We still having lunch tomorrow, Jerry? Looks like Carl Denton tested positive for marijuana. That moves Cush solidly up to numero uno in the draft.

DOOLER

Oh, that'll really help this party! Let's all talk business!

JERRY

Dooler, you know Bob Sugar.

SUGAR

The best commercial director in the business. I hail you.

DOOLER

Sorry I yelled. You have exquisite taste.

SUGAR
(exiting)

Everybody's having a great time. You're both nuts – the movie's great.

DOOLER

I like that guy.

(*The movie, which plays simultaneously with the conversation, is a Hi-8 confessional of Jerry's former girlfriends. Michael Jordan is cut into this, nodding, as if he were actually interviewing. The effect is funny, but the confessions are brutally honest. All seem to agree on some basic points. Jerry always has a girlfriend. Hates to be alone. Many met him on the first day he'd broken up with the last one. The relationship always competes with his job, and the job always wins.*

He is good at friendship, bad at intimacy. Sequence ends with Avery in character, wielding a blowtorch, threatening to burn all these old phone numbers. Ending is a good-natured montage of photos, many embarrassing, cut to music.)

JERRY
(wounded good sport)

. . . this is . . . uh . . . too funny . . .

DOOLER

They're not laughing, man. Something's wrong.

INT. SMI OFFICE – DAY

Elevator doors open. Maguire is now paranoid. He walks through the buzzing SMI headquarters, heading for his corner office. He is like an

FBI man searching treetops and corners for the gunman. Everywhere he looks is a potential Grassy Knoll. He passes an agent having an emotional hallway conversation with a baseball player, bends down to check the sheet of slides being approved by a large but seated basketball player. He is always moving forward. There is trouble in the air, but only he seems to sense it. He turns the corner and is met by his assistant Wendy, who hands him a long list of calls.

WENDY

(as in 'get ready')

Marcee's here. She's already in your office, and she's late for her plane back to Phoenix.

JERRY

Thanks, Wendy.

INT. JERRY MAGUIRE'S OFFICE – DAY

Jerry enters his corner office overlooking both the shiny waters of Newport Beach and a large mall parking lot. Already standing, reading the mail on his desk is lively Marcee Tidwell. African-American, gorgeous, a heat-seeking smartbomb. She is also newly pregnant.

MARCEE

Jerry, Rod is very, very upset. Tyson, no!

Across the room, four-year-old menace, Tyson, ceases trying to pry a Plexiglas case off the wall.

JERRY

Tyson, hello.

Tyson just stares at Jerry. Jerry has little luck with kids. He gives Marcee a quick peck and heads for the fridge. He grabs a two-pint bottle of orange Gatorade – another habit – and sits down at his desk. He slips into crisis mode like an old shirt.

JERRY

How can I make your life better?

MARCEE

This is humiliating, Jerry. Where is our offer from Arizona? My husband is the fastest, fiercest, most explosive, raddest

55

wide-receiver in the league. Now I don't know what you do for your four percent –

The door opens, Bob Sugar pokes his head in.

SUGAR

Cronin's okay for lunch?

JERRY

Marcee – this is one of our agents. This is Bob Sugar, who needs to learn to knock.

SUGAR

Pleasure.

MARCEE

You've called our house, right?

SUGAR
(*exiting*)
Sorry to interrupt you guys.

MARCEE

. . . now I don't know what you do for your four percent, but this man, my husband, has a whole plan, an image . . . and when you put him in a Waterbed Warehouse commercial, excuse me, you are making him common! When we deserve the big four – shoe, car, clothing-line, soft drink. The four jewels on the celebrity endorsement dollar.

JERRY

Wow.

MARCEE

Majored in marketing, baby, and so did my husband.

The desk buzzes, and Jerry ignores it. She commands the best in him.

MARCEE

You gonna get that –

JERRY

Not a chance.

(*as she smiles*)

Marcee, things are changing around here. I'll be able to give you and Rod a little more attention.

> MARCEE
> Damn right, and you can start by taking Rod's poster and putting it where people can see it!

> JERRY
> (*it's infectious*)
> Damn right.

He climbs up on the edge of his sofa, and reaches for the poster with his hanging device. True to Marcee's complaint, the poster hangs in the Upper Siberian region of his wall.

> MARCEE
> Look at that handsome man, trying to build a life up there by the air conditioner. We're coming to get ya, darlin'!

ON THE POSTER – CLOSE

It is the kind of poster that is strictly the domain of the second-tier player. Commanding wide-receiver Rod Tidwell, twenty-seven, stands shirtless, hands on hips, looking vaguely uncomfortable. Emblazoned above his head: IN ROD WE TRUST. *Elsewhere in the room, we hear the inevitable crash.* (*'Tyson!'*)

EXT. CRONIN'S GRILL – AFTERNOON

Crowded outdoor restaurant in the business district. Jerry sits down opposite Bob Sugar, still making a few notes.

> JERRY
> Tidwell contract . . . new glass cabinet.

> SUGAR
> You okay?

> JERRY
> (*looking up*)
> I'm fine. What's up?

> SUGAR
> I came here to let you go.

57

                              JERRY
    Pardon me?

                              SUGAR
    Came here to fire you, Jerry.

For a long moment there is only silence.

    It's real, Jerry. You . . . you should say something.

Suddenly he's flushed, a little embarrassed.

                              JERRY
    Aw, shit . . . the crowded restaurant . . . so there's no
    scene . . .

                              SUGAR
    I know. It sucks. I *suck.*

*In a back room, the waiters are singing the restaurant's 'Birthday Song'
to someone else. Jerry is dying.*

                              JERRY
    You . . .

                              SUGAR
                          (*razor sharp*)
    You did this to yourself. *You* said 'fewer clients'. You put it
    all on paper. Scully was very upset. He sent me to do this. I
    agreed. Heart attacks make some people sweeter, but not
    him. You did this to *yourself* –

Jerry's mouth opens to finish his sentence, but Sugar continues.

    – although I do gotta hand it to you. For about five minutes
    you had everyone applauding smaller revenues.

*Maguire reaches for water. The sound of ice cubes clinking is suddenly
very loud to him. He is drowning.*

                              JERRY
    You . . . ungrateful . . . unctuous . . .

                              SUGAR
                          (*ever unctuous*)
    . . . dick?

                               58

JERRY

Dick.

SUGAR

Give me a little credit for doing this face to face! What I went
through knowing I was going to do this to my mentor! Can
you get past *yourself* a second?

JERRY

You'll lose.

SUGAR
(*musically*)

You wanted smaller.

JERRY

I'm over it. Now I want all my clients and yours, too.

SUGAR

Jerry –

JERRY

– and I'll get 'em.

SUGAR

Okay, whatever, you'll always be my hero, Jerry. Always
always always. We're bringing other elements in, we're
focusing on endorsements – it's not about handholding
anymore. We're no longer babysitters –

*Jerry fights the desire to use his fists. Hangs on to the table. He's
starting to freak out now. Trying to stay calm. Sugar's mouth keeps
moving, but all we hear is the rising music in Jerry's mind.*

EXT. STREET – DAY

*Jerry tries to move briskly down the street, through the lunchtime
businessmen traffic. Back to the office.*

EXT. CRONIN'S – DAY

Sugar dines alone now. Casually whips out a portable phone.

INT. SMI ELEVATOR – DAY

Jerry in the elevator, eyes wide, mind racing. Dorothy Boyd sees him, raises a hand to say hello. Decides this is not a good time.

INT. JERRY'S OFFICE – DAY

Maguire rolls the fax machine over to his desk. He takes a breath, lines up his phone book and his Powerbook, and goes to work, dialing. Next to his hand is a client list. Top of the list is Frank Cushman. He speed-dials, gets a busy signal.

INT. CUSHMAN HOME/ODESSA – DAY

Frank 'Cush' Cushman picks up the phone. He's playing NBA Jam on his Gameboy as he talks. His girlfriend, Anne-Louise, sits in the background.

>   CUSH
> This is Cush.

EXT. CRONIN'S – DAY

>   SUGAR
> Cush. Hey, Dudeboy! It's Bob Sugar. Listen, I'm callin' ya
> first 'cause you're the most important guy in sports . . .

INT. JERRY'S OFFICE – DAY

Maguire on the telephone, fighting hard, as he sends a fax.

>   JERRY
> Carla, right now you're paying 25 percent of your
> endorsements to SMI, I would cut my commission by seven
> percent . . .

He takes a stack of his Mission Statements and sentences them to the bottom drawer.

EXT. BACK YARD – DAY

Supersonics star Gary Payton holds a cellular.

PAYTON
Run that by me one more time.

EXT. STREET – DAY

Sugar strolls back to the office, talking on the portable.

SUGAR
You read that memo I snuck to you, the guy's tired of the job.
Tired of making you money.

INT. JERRY'S OFFICE – DAY

Maguire feeds a fax, types another fax on his Powerbook.

JERRY
And when I got you that big contract in Chicago, and the fan
poll in the *Sun-Times* was 93 percent against you, who went
and found you that sympathetic journalist who turned it all
around, it was me . . .

INT. SUGAR'S OFFICE – DAY

Several other agents working the cause behind Sugar.

SUGAR
He's costing you money, Debra . . . He's old-school.

INT. JERRY'S OFFICE – DAY

Jerry on the toilet/ Not a minute to spare.

JERRY
. . . SMI represents all three quarterbacks on your team,
where's their loyalty going to be? You stay with me, I'd fight
for *you* alone. You'd be my only client on that team . . .

INT. SUGAR'S OFFICE – DAY

Several other agents help in background, as he rips through calls.

SUGAR
I got the clients. I got the juice.

62

JERRY

Sukreet, we've spent quality time together, and not just at
your arraignment.

INT. SMI OFFICE – DAY

*Dorothy walks the center aisle with some contracts. To the right and left
of her the phones are ringing. Something is amiss. She stops at the desk
of fellow Accounts Exec Cleo, thirty-two.*

DOROTHY

What's going on?

CLEO
(*no big deal*)
They fired Jerry Maguire. Did it at Cronin's.

*Dorothy groans softly, as she lowers herself into her seat. She is strangely
affected by the news. She scoots back on her roller-chair, and looks down
the hallway to Maguire's office door.*

INT. JERRY'S OFFICE – DAY

JERRY

– personal attention –

INT. SUGAR'S OFFICE – DAY

SUGAR

– more money, more endorsements –

INT. JERRY'S OFFICE – DAY

JERRY

– a family of athletes –

INT. SUGAR'S OFFICE – DAY

SUGAR

– the millennium, eight hundred channels, more
endorsements.

INT. JERRY'S OFFICE – DAY

> JERRY
> (*intimate, a friend*)
> Kathy! Hi, it's Jerry Maguire. Boy, what a day . . .

INT. REHEARSAL ROOM – DAY

Kathy Sanders, twenty-two-year-old figure skater, sits on a couch. Kathy's adoring mom and dad sit next to her, listening in on the extension.

> KATHY
> (*anguished*)
> I already heard from Bob Sugar. Jerry, I want to cry for what they did to you at SMI. You helped me win that gold at the Olympics, we have history, and . . . oh, Jerry . . . if we weren't in the middle of the Acura deal, you know I'd go with you! Oh, Jerry, oh, God . . .

As she begins to fully break down, there is a clock on the line. She is pained and outraged at the interruption.

> . . . Call-waiting . . . who could be calling me *now*? . . .

She clicks the phone once. Her voice is suddenly cheery.

> Hiyee.

INT. JERRY'S OFFICE

> JERRY
> Still me, Kathy.

She instantly starts 'crying' again.

> KATHY
> Ohhhhhhhh . . .

INT. SUGAR'S OFFICE – DUSK

Sugar crosses off another name on his list. Pace accelerating.

It's not show 'friends'. It's show *business*. Think about it.

He hangs up, as a Junior Agent (Rick) hands him another cellular. Quietly:

RICK

Kelly Wellman.

SUGAR

. . . hi, Kelly . . .

INT. JERRY'S OFFICE – DUSK

Jerry on the phone.

JERRY

Rod! How ya doing? Jerry Maguire.

INTERCUT WITH:

INT. TIDWELL KITCHEN/HOUSE – DUSK

Rod Tidwell, twenty-seven, is a powerful, compact physical presence. He fixes young son Tyson an early supper as he talks. In the background, monitoring the crisis, is Marcee Tidwell. (There is construction in progress in Tidwell's ramshackle desert house.)

TIDWELL

'How am I doing?' I'll tell you. I'm sweatin', dude! That's how I'm 'doin'. I'm sweatin' my contract. I'm sweatin' Bob Sugar calling and telling me I'm blowing the big endorsements if I stay with you. I'm sweatin'. You hear what I'm saying?

JERRY

I hear what you're saying . . .

TIDWELL

No. I hear that you hear what I'm saying. But do you *hear what I'm saying*?

65

INT. SUGAR'S OFFICE — SAME TIME

Sugar works off a wristwatch. He spends no longer than three minutes on each call.

SUGAR

. . . I'll bet he hasn't even called you yet, right, Jennifer? Wait, I need to cough . . .

He covers the phone, as Rick hands him a cellular with another call on it.

RICK

Ben Bixby.

Rick then takes over for Jennifer.

SUGAR

. . . Hi, Ben, hold on a second, you haven't heard from Maguire? You *haven't*? Well, that tells you a lot. Wait, I need to cough.

RICK
(*handing another phone*)

Your mother.

SUGAR

Fuck her, call back.

INT. JERRY'S OFFICE

Jerry is still on the same Tidwell call. Looking at his watch. Phone bank blinking in the shot.

JERRY

Rod, can't we get into this in person?

TIDWELL

Didn't you tell my wife more attention?

JERRY

Yes. I did.

TIDWELL

Good, 'cause we're just getting started on my list of things you need to know. Take notes if you want to.

66

INT. TIDWELL HALLWAY – NIGHT

Tidwell walks down the hallway, past clippings and citations from his career. Marcee follows, always listening.

> TIDWELL
> See . . . I am a valuable commodity. I go *across the middle*. I
> see the ball and a dude coming right at me, wanting to kill
> me, I tell my brain 'Get killed, catch the ball.' Boo-ya!
> Touchdown! I make miracles happen! That's New York
> Steak, baby. Rare. And yet, nobody's giving me *props*.
> Nobody's giving me *love*. Nobody. I went to Arizona State,
> I'm from Arizona, I break Arizona records, I'm a Sun Devil,
> man!!!

> JERRY
> Now you want Arizona dollars.

> TIDWELL
> Exactly. And I'm sitting here with an ant problem, look! And
> my brother Tee Pee's room is flooded with water. Say hello to
> Jerry Maguire –

We meet Tee Pee, twenty-four. Tee Pee, who lives free of charge in Rod's house, is a nakedly jealous and more political version of his brother. He says into the phone:

> TEE PEE
> Hello, brother Maguire.

Tidwell takes the phone back, and continues through the house, with Tee Pee now following the procession of family monitoring the important call. Meanwhile, Jerry sees the lights on the phone bank going out.

> TIDWELL
> – the house is fallin' apart, we don't even know where we're
> gonna live in a year, and I'm supposed to be a 'superstar',
> man!

Jerry looks at his watch. Doomed.

> JERRY
> I need a decision from you, Rod.

INT. SUGAR'S OFFICE — NIGHT

Sugar has three phones going, as Junior Agent Rick feeds him calls.

> SUGAR
> . . . killer, Steve, good decision.
>> (*next call*)
> So it's yes, right? Excellente.
>> (*next call*)
> Tell me it's yes . . . yes? *Yes!*

INT. BEDROOM — NIGHT

Tidwell enters bedroom. Takes off his shoes, adds them to an enormous collection. Marcee, Tyson and Tee Pee in tow.

> TIDWELL
> – now to recap, I want to stay in Arizona, I want the new contract, I like you, you're nice to my wife, *I will stay with you*, that's what I'm doing for you, but here's what you're gonna do for me. You listening?

Jerry has now given up trying to steer this conversation. Elsewhere in the office, he hears someone's noise of celebration. Through the window, he sees the forces that have just about killed him.

> JERRY
>> (*dying*)
> Mmm. Hmm.

> TIDWELL
> It's a very personal, very important thing. It's a family motto. So I want to share it with you. You ready?

> JERRY
> I'm ready.

> TIDWELL
> 'Show me the money.' Show. Me. The. *Money.*

> JERRY
> I got it.

TIDWELL

Now doesn't that just make you feel *good* to say it? Say it with me.

Jerry sits in the oncoming darkness, watching the blinking white lights on the phone bank on the desk.

JERRY

Show. Me. The. Money.

TIDWELL

Congratulations. You're still my agent.

Tidwell hangs up. Nearby, Tee Pee shakes his head.

TEE PEE

An African-American man running with a little ball, working for white owners and white agents. It's the iconography of racism . . .
(*off Tidwell's dismissive look*)
But I woulda stayed at the bigger company.

INT. SUGAR'S OFFICE – NIGHT

Sugar crosses the last call off his sheet, and throws himself on the sofa with a soft poof. The younger turks watch their new leader. Victory is his.

INT. JERRY'S OFFICE – NIGHT

Jerry stands at the door, holding some belongings. He looks back and symbolically flips the light switch off. Unfortunately he hasn't realized the lights are already off. So, in his final gesture, surprising himself, he has weirdly turned the lights on.

EXT. CORNER OFFICE – NIGHT

Bam. Jerry's door opens. He exits his office with box. Many of the other agents now try not to watch him leaving.

JERRY

Well, don't worry! I'm not going to do what you think I'm going to do, which is *flip out!*

69

Jerry goes to a water dispenser, calming himself, and fills a small Dixie cup. Downs it and fills it again, rubbing his face.

But let me just say, as I ease out of the office I helped build – sorry, but it's a fact –

ON DOROTHY

Watching from her cubicle.

BACK TO JERRY.

> JERRY
> – that there is such a thing as manners. A way of treating people . . .
> *(notices fish tank)*
> These fish have manners! They have *manners.*

And now Jerry feels bravado, mixed with a wave of anger. Another cup of water as he finds power.

In fact. They're coming with me! I'm starting a new company, and the fish will come with me and . . . you can *call me sentimental.*

He begins dipping into the tank, grabbing the one exotic fish that failed to escape his cup. He grabs a Baggie from an assistant's desk, shakes out some crumbs, and dumps the fish inside.

> *(to fish)*
> . . . it's okay . . . it's okay . . .

Nearby, a Xerox repair guy watches the human train wreck.

But if anybody else wants to come with me, this moment will be the ground floor of something real and fun and inspiring and true in this godforsaken business and we will do it together! Who's coming with me besides . . . Flipper here?

But clearly even Flipper is not happy with the new arrangement.

Anybody going with me?

Silence, someone coughs. Maguire's lid is blowing off.

Wendy? Shall we?

WENDY

I'm three months away from the pay increase, Jerry. I have to, uh . . . you know, stay.

Jerry absorbs the blow, and takes the keys from the top of her desk. She can't look at him. Jerry stands alone, the blue Mission Statement on Wendy's desk sits accusingly IN FRAME. *There is only silence now, the loudest kind.*

JERRY

Okay, anybody else?

ON DOROTHY

She looks around. Doesn't anybody believe in the very thing they were applauding three days ago? She has an odd reaction, a muscle twitch of the soul. Before she knows it, she stands boldly, unfortunately knocking a cup of coffee on to herself in the process.

DOROTHY

I'll go with you.
> (*quietly, on her coffee stain*)

Wonderful . . .

She dabs at her pants. Next to her, Cleo looks on sadly.

JERRY

Dorothy Boyd! Thank you!

She gathers her things, increasingly aware of what she's done, as the wild-eyed figure from across the hall moves closer to her.

We will see you all again. Sleep tight.

He walks to Dorothy, and together they exit down the hallway corridor.

WIDE SHOT: *For the first time, we see the full expanse of the huge SMI headquarters. And down in the corner of the frame, two small figures leave carrying boxes.*

> (*to Dorothy*)

Let's see how they do without us.

A beat of silence, then noise returns to its normal commercial roar. A couple of fleas have been swatted off the carcass of an immense beast.

INT. ELEVATOR – NIGHT

The tragic-sounding beep of the elevator passing floors. Jerry Maguire stands with Dorothy, both still charged with adrenalin. And then the first pangs of dread. There is silence. The elevator stops. A young, amorous Couple enter. Both are about twenty-four, and the guy presses a number five flights down. In a moment, we realize they are deaf. They sign to each other, murmuring noises of love. And then the guy signs something, obviously powerful, because the girl emits a delighted gasp, as does Dorothy. The couple are truly in their own world. They kiss before exiting on their floor. And suddenly the elevator seems empty without them.

JERRY

Wonder what he said.

DOROTHY

My favorite aunt is deaf. He said, 'You complete me.'

INT. BUILDING LOBBY – NIGHT

Jerry and Dorothy pass through another office's party. Loud music.

Jerry and Dorothy walk to their cars.

> DOROTHY
> So I know this is a bad time, but – you *will* have a medical program, right?

> JERRY
> Sure. Yes. Medical, I don't know.

He spaces out for a moment. Awkwardly, she touches him briefly.

> DOROTHY
> And I guess we didn't talk about money. So, I'll just dive in –

> JERRY
> Give me your number. I'll call tomorrow. I'm just a little. I'm a little insane right now.
> > (*off her look*)
> But it's going to be great.

> DOROTHY
> No no, I know –

They arrive at her red Camry. She writes her number on the back of a business card.

> JERRY
> But I mean really . . . wonderfully . . .
> > (*out of steam*)
> . . . great.

> DOROTHY
> Absolutely.

She climbs into her car, rolls down the window.

> JERRY
> And when you think about what you've done later, don't panic.

> DOROTHY
> Me? No. My sister – it's a good bet.

She starts the engine.

That took guts.

> JERRY
>
> Same to you.

She salutes him as she drives off. His own move, played back to him.
Camera moves away from Jerry, as he stands alone in the parking lot.
Salutes her in return. Herb Alpert: 'The Lonely Bull'. Stripped of
power, his once mighty theme now seems puny.

FADE TO:

EXT. DOROTHY'S HOME – NIGHT

Lights glow inside this small but cozy home on a side street in
Manhattan Beach. Windows open. The sound of women's voices.

INT. LIVING ROOM – NIGHT

A living room filled with ten earnest, talkative divorced women. We
meet Jan, thirty, who speaks shyly, thoughtfully, covering her braces
often as she speaks. She holds a too-full glass of red wine. (Much of the
talk in this women's group will be improved by our cast of actresses.)

> JAN
>
> I love men. I respect men. But that doesn't change the fact
> that most of them belong in cages.

The other nine women nod with deep understanding.

INT. KITCHEN – NIGHT

Dorothy does the dishes. Across the room, Laurel has her nightly
cigarette, blowing smoke out the window. They are in mid-argument.

> LAUREL
>
> What about medical?

> DOROTHY
>
> Of course, medical!

LAUREL
(*unconvinced*)
You are a single mother. You have given up the right to be
frivolous.

DOROTHY
(*irritated*)
If you'd read what he wrote, you would have left with him,
too. And I can always take that job in San Diego.

LAUREL
(*more irritated*)
You know how much those Well Child exams cost –

DOROTHY
(*overlapping*)
Of course I know –

LAUREL/DOROTHY
A hundred and fifty dollars.

LAUREL
And that's just when he's well –

DOROTHY
Wait. *Where is Ray?*

LAUREL
He's in the living room, asleep.

Dorothy dries her hands, flicking in a hurry.

DOROTHY
Wonderful. Next time you lecture me, don't leave my little
boy in a room with your divorced women's group . . .

*She exits in a hurry, as Laurel throws her cigarette into the garbage
disposal and grinds.*

LAUREL
Sorry.

INT. LIVING ROOM – NIGHT

Ray dreams sweetly in the middle of this rockbed of women's woes.

76

Dorothy strokes his head, as she plucks him up. In frame another woman, Alice, fifty, speaks passionately to the group.

> ALICE
> (*sweet smile*)
> . . . okay, I've finally, *finally*, found anger here. I can see Carl right, now and I can finally tell him –

> DOROTHY

Shhhh!

Dorothy exits, protectively stroking her son's head.

Come on, buddy, we're going to bed.

INT. HALLWAY – NIGHT

She stops for a moment, little boy in her hands. The enormity of the day arrives with a thud.

> DOROTHY
> (*to herself*)

What did I do?

INT. JERRY'S BEDROOM – NIGHT

Maguire rifles through his closet. Avery stands in the background, studying him carefully.

> JERRY
> The power move is to go unannounced.
> *(sotto)*
> Black suit, right?

> AVERY
> *(sotto)*
> And the Egyptian cotton shirt that works with or without the tie.
> *(full volume)*
> Tell me again, how was it left with Cush?

Jerry yanks the suit from the closet, offering a perfect imitation of Cush.

> JERRY
> 'Dad says we gawn sleep on it.'

> AVERY
> Function function function. Forward motion is everything.

JERRY

Seventy-two clients. *One* stayed.
> (*sotto*)

Jacket on, tie in pocket.

AVERY

Good.
> (*full volume*)

They're all heatseekers! All of them, everybody.

JERRY

Everybody.

AVERY

You go to Texas. You keep one superstar and they'll all
follow. There's no real loyalty, and the first person who told
me that, Jerry Maguire, was *you*.

JERRY

I think I was trying to sleep with you at the time.

AVERY

Well, it worked, and I will not let you fail. You are Jerry Ma-
fuckin-guire.

JERRY

That's right.

AVERY

King of Housecalls! Master of the Living Room!

JERRY

Okay, this is working.

AVERY

You are not a *loser*.

*Jerry stops, turns. This word is very, very new to him. Especially when
applied to himself.*

JERRY

Who said anything about 'loser'?

AVERY

I'm sorry, I was on a roll –

JERRY

You said 'loser'.

AVERY

Mistake. I meant something else. When do you want to leave?

Jerry zips his bag shut. He is packed and ready.

JERRY

Now

AVERY

Let's go. I'll drive you.

JERRY
(*stops, an odd thought*)

What if I don't get him?

Avery takes his bag, they head for the door.

AVERY
(*her mantra*)

Function function function. Forward motion is everything.
Cush saves all.

AIRPLANE WHEELS – NIGHT

folding up.

EXT. TEXAS ROAD/INT. RENT-A-CAR – MORNING

Jerry drives the bumpiest Texas backroad ever.

EXT. CUSHMAN DOOR – DAY

Jerry exits car. Adjusts the jacket. Scared. Takes the tie off, too, returns to the car and tosses it inside. He walks to the front door with strange anticipation. Suddenly an intercom crackles, jolting him with a booming and cheerful voice:

MATT CUSHMAN
(*voice-over*)

No sports agents allowed! Ha ha.

Jerry spots the small electronic camera pointed at him from the upper corner of this rustic home. The door buzzes.

INT. CUSHMAN HALLWAY/DEN – DAY

Jerry follows the voice down a hallway loaded with Cushabilia.

> MATT CUSHMAN
> (*voice-over*)
> I'm in the back den, Jerry.

He moves into the den, finding Matt Cushman, forty, who stands at the living room bar. He is a former athlete, now a J. Crew cowboy.

> MATT
> You like a Bloody Beer, Jerry? Beer and tomato juice –

> JERRY
> No thanks.
> (*takes a breath*)
> Matt, I came here because, in all honesty, your son is just another piece of cattle to SMI. But to me –

> MATT
> (*overlapping*)
> We decided to stay with you.

On pure instinct, he hugs Matt Cushman.

> JERRY
> Oh, thank you.

> MATT
> Told myself – if he shows up, we'll stick with him.

> JERRY
> You know, I'm not a hugger and yet . . . I can't let go.

Matt laughs, as Cush lopes in from the kitchen. Little brother Keith, fourteen, enters with him.

> CUSH
> Hey, Jerry, what's been going on?

Cush, Matt and Jerry brainstorm around the ceremonial 'wagon wheel table' where decisions are made in this house.

> MATT
>
> I want him to go number one in the draft, and I want him to play.

> JERRY
>
> It's either going to be Denver or San Diego trading up to take him.

> CUSH
> (*big grin*)
>
> Hell, I'll either surf or ski. I don't care.

> MATT
>
> Denver is where he should be.

> JERRY
>
> I'll give it everything.

> MATT
>
> You know I don't do 'contracts'. But'cha do have my word, and it's stronger than oak.

Jerry toasts Matt with a bloody beer. A good day.

INT. RENT-A-CAR/TEXAS – DAY

Jerry drives back on the same bumpy road. On the radio is a Rolling Stones song he thinks he knows.

> JERRY
> (*sings*)
>
> Feelin' . . .

He realizes he doesn't know the words at all. He switches channels. Finds a Rush song, with ornate lyrics. No one will ever know what the words are. Switches again. All he wants is to sing along with a song he knows. Finally he finds Tom Petty and the Heartbreakers' 'Refugee'. He drives through the countryside, singing the call and response of the song, like a happy idiot.

INT. DALLAS/FORT WORTH AIRPORT – DAY

Jerry turns into shot. He's on the pay phone. He's jacked.

> JERRY
> Dorothy? Jerry Maguire! Is Avery there? Where can I reach
> her?

INTERCUT WITH:

INT. DOROTHY/LAUREL'S HOUSE – DAY

*Dorothy is at her home work desk. Curious and nervous about the new
arrangement. In the back room, the drier shakes the house.*

> DOROTHY
> Uh, she had to fly to Atlanta, didn't leave me her hotel
> number.

*Through the back kitchen door comes neighbor and surrogate dad,
Chad, twenty-five. He's with Ray, who holds pieces of wood and a
hammer.*

> CHAD
> The new playhouse rocks, Dotty.

> RAY
> *(jumping)*
> Yeah!

> DOROTHY
> Honey – later, okay?
> *(as Ray jumps on her)*
> Whoop. Wait.

> JERRY
> Hello?

> DOROTHY
> *(back to phone)*
> Sorry, that's my son and the nanny.

Chad shares a look with Laurel. Nanny?

DOROTHY

I had the calls transferred to my home so I could go over your
stuff.

*Chad now notices the slightly excited tone in her demeanor. He sits
down nearby and listens to her talk to Maguire.*

JERRY

No, that's fine. What calls came in today?

DOROTHY

Wait. That's yesterday, from the other office. Today is . . .

*She flips the call record from yesterday – 150 calls – to today, which is
blank.*

DOROTHY

. . . light.

JERRY

Shit, it's just so frustrating to not be able to talk to Avery –

She zips through her laptop.

DOROTHY

Wait a minute, it has to be one of the NFL hotels we do
business with – let me look – but in the meantime, about this
job –

JERRY
(*importantly*)

Dorothy, let me tell you something, we are *back*. We are so
very very back. *I re-signed Cush.* We're set.

DOROTHY

We are?

JERRY

It's all going to work.

DOROTHY

I just got goosebumps.

JERRY
(*manic, quiet*)
It's all going to work. We're going to save the world.

DOROTHY
Well, I'm happy for you.

JERRY
Happy for us.

Oddly, the phrase affects her physically.

DOROTHY
Happy for *us* . . . okay. Here's the number. 404-453-2222.

JERRY
Thanks. Gotta go.

She catches herself hanging on the telephone.

DOROTHY
Okay. Call me later, hon.

She hangs up, and looks over to Laurel and Chad. Both of them stare at her.

DOROTHY
Wait. Did I just say 'hon' to him?
(*as they nod*)
Twenty-six years old. I'm already saying 'hon'. Hug your mother quickly –

Ray hugs his mother. Chad looks at her, something is different about Dorothy. Laurel walks away, sharing a look with Chad.

INT. DALLAS AIRPORT – DAY

Jerry is now teeming with energy, professional and sexual.

JERRY
Avery, I signed Cush. Again.

INTERCUT WITH:

INT. ATLANTA HOTEL SUITE – DAY

Avery in mid-conference with four other NFL men in background.

> AVERY

YA-HOOOO-SIE!

She falls back into a chair, kicking her expensive shoes on to the bed. In the background we see the hungry look of her male co-workers. Part of them lusts after her. The larger part knows she would demolish them, and pick her teeth with their bones.

> JERRY

I know. Sorry I threw a scare into our lives there –

> AVERY

Don't worry about it – I never told you what I thought of that *memo* either.

> JERRY

Well, no, you didn't –

> AVERY

You lost your head, it happens.
> (*quickly*)
I'm so *fuckin'* jazzed! Listen. I'm stuck here, how 'bout if you meet me here and we all fly into New York together for the draft?

> JERRY

It's a plan –

> AVERY

I'll set it up with your girl. Woo! This is when it's good, Jerry. Enjoy it. Live it. Love it. And when I see you, I'm going to give you the best blow job of your life.

He hangs up, staring at the phone. In the room with Avery, the co-workers look at each other. She is far, far out of their league.

INT. DOROTHY'S CAR – LATER MORNING – DRIVING

Dorothy Boyd speeds Jerry to the airport, the electricity fills the car. On the radio, a sports station debates the future of Cushman, as Jerry whips

through a stack of sports pages and talks on the phone at the same time.
Ray sits in the back seat.

> JERRY

Rod! Jerry Maguire. I'm on my way to the draft right now.
Personal attention! Here we go. There will be about ten hours
tomorrow where I'm the hottest agent on earth, because of
Cushman. I want you to come with us. Just be there. I want
you to meet some other teams, get your profile up. Great.
Dorothy will call you with the ticket. We'll meet in Atlanta.

Hangs up.

> DOROTHY

Avery'll meet you at B gate at four-fifteen. Don't be late.

> RAY

Jerry, do you know the human head weighs eight pounds?

> JERRY
> *(nods, to Ray)*

Do you know that Troy Aikman, in only six years, has passed
for over 16,303 yards?

> RAY

Do you know bees and dogs can smell fear?

> DOROTHY

Oh, I put Tidwell on the same floor at the Marriott Marquis.
He doesn't smoke, does he?

> JERRY

No idea –
> *(to Ray, now playing trivia)*

Did you know the career record for most hits is 4,256 by Pete
Rose, who is *not* in the hall of fame?

> RAY

Do you know my next-door neighbor has three rabbits?

> JERRY
> *(to Dorothy)*

I can't compete with that.

She's a little giddy over his rapport with Ray. She touches Maguire briefly on the shoulder, then immediately pulls away, embarrassed. He doesn't even notice.

> DOROTHY
> Okay, have we gone over everything? Back on Tuesday, right?

> JERRY
> Yep. Have a good time at school, Ray. Wish me luck.

> DOROTHY/RAY
> (*together*)
> Luck!

Jerry exits smiling. They watch him inch into the crowded airport. Into frame, obscuring their view, enters another couple, who embrace each other and their small boy. It's a genuinely sweet goodbye, and we linger on Dorothy and Ray who both watch with private fantasies of the goodbye they didn't get. Mother and son look at each other, communicating volumes. They pull back into traffic.

INT. ATLANTA AIRPORT – DAY

Tidwell watches as Jerry arrives late at the B Gate in Atlanta. Avery, tall and cool in plaid skirt and shades, is in combat mode. Nearby, Cush is surrounded by fans and fawning airline employees. Tidwell looks jealous and ignored as he leans against the airline counter, unnoticed. A lone Kid approaches Tidwell.

> KID
> Are you Hootie?

> TIDWELL
> (*irritated*)
> No, man, I'm not Hootie

Kid leaves disappointed. Tidwell sinks lower. Doesn't anyone know his stardom, his essence, his power?

> BOARDING ANNOUNCEMENT
> (*voice-over*)
> All those disabled, and Frank Cushman, can board now . . .

INT. AIRPLANE – DAY

Jerry sits next to Cushman, who is reading Bukowski's Notes of a
Dirty Old Man. *Tidwell sits next to Avery. They are a small family,
and Jerry feels at home with his operation. Matt, Keith and Anne-
Louise sit behind them. Suddenly Cush looks up with a big thought.*

CUSH
(*a big thought*)
Jerry. Why does God sometimes reward the evil and punish
the good?

*Jerry shares a look with Avery, who is on the other side of Cush. Her
stockings swish as she crosses her legs.*

JERRY
Let me think about that. Want something to drink?

CUSH
(*thoughtful pause*)
I see what you're saying.

JERRY
Wait. What do you mean?

*The two men have now totally confused each other. Tidwell leans across
the aisle to Cush, attempting camaraderie.*

TIDWELL
Hey, man, I wish I had a quarterback like you in Arizona.
You're the *shit*.

Cush looks up. Compliments blow off him like a summer breeze.

CUSH
Thank ya.

*Tidwell waits for a compliment of his own, but Cush doesn't offer one.
He returns to the book. Tidwell feels slighted.*

TIDWELL
(*loud mumble*)
Well, you ain't *that* mothafuckin' good.

CUSH

Say what?

TIDWELL

I said – last I heard, Jesus Christ was still in Heaven. And you ain't even played in the NFL.

Cush throws his book away, ready for anything, as Tidwell rises. Nearby passengers begin to panic.

JERRY

This can't be happening to me.

AVERY

Jerry! Do something –

Jerry throws himself in front of Cushman.

JERRY

HEY. Knock it off. What are you, five years old? Am I taking the kids to Chuck E. Cheese here? Grow up, both of you! We are a family. And we go to the draft in an orderly fashion.

Jerry wonders if he's pushed his meal tickets around too much.

TIDWELL

Hey, man, I *did* Chuck E. Cheese.

CUSH

Me too, dude. Especially that big old singin' Elvis Monkey. That's just *insanity*, man.

TIDWELL

Heard that.

Tidwell and Cush exchange a fingertips five. Briefly, the two clients bond. Past Tidwell, Avery smiles engagingly at Jerry. He handled the situation well. She crosses her legs, stockings swishing. The workplace excites her.

EXT. MARRIOTT MARQUIS – NIGHT

The buzzing headquarters for the NFL draft. Limo doors open and out pours Maguire and company. Media lights flick on, bathing Cush. Reporters chatter. Fans at the outskirts are calling out to the young star

(*'Go get the big chi-ching, Cush!'*). *Avery smoothly pulls ESPN into the front position. All the Reporters ask the same question – 'Will it be San Diego or Denver?' Telegenic Cush shrugs and smiles.* (*'I'll either surf or ski.'*) *Jerry answers carefully, all the while watching Avery do her job with peak efficiency. There is nothing more attractive than a person burningly efficient at their job. Shot drifts off this media bubble to find Tidwell watching, ignored at the outskirts. Around him, the pools of media light surround the other players and big-shots. He exits unnoticed.*

TIDWELL
(*mumbles to himself*)

Pleasure talking with you all . . . always a pleasure . . .

INT. GIFT SHOP – NIGHT (LATER)

Tidwell hides out in a nearby gift shop, thumbing through magazines. The chip on his shoulder grows by the minute. Elsewhere in the gift shop, he notices a young athlete and his mother. Both wear self-promoting colorful homemade T-shirts with the young athlete's face on it. Something about them, their pure enthusiasm, rubs Tidwell in an odd way. He almost cries, for himself, for humanity, as Jerry enters. Tidwell is embarrassed to have been caught in this misty state.

JERRY

At last I find you.

TIDWELL
(*sharply*)

Why the fuck am I here? I feel like I'm five years late for the prom.

In a look, Jerry sizes up the situation. With a hand on Tidwell's large shoulder, he smoothly pumps up the big man's ego. He guides them back out on to Times Square, back to the hotel.

Nobody gives a damn about me being here.

JERRY

Come on. Come with me. We're going back to the hotel, we're going to take a walk through this lobby. I want every media guy, every player rep, everybody to see you for what you are. The best-kept secret in the NFL. The most commanding wide-receiver in the game. Fast. Fierce. Wildly charismatic. You ready? Let's do it.

He is privately thrilled, but offers only:

TIDWELL
(*begrudgingly*)

A'right. Let's walk.

We hear the ripping Guitar explosion of The Who's 'Magic Bus' from Live at Leeds.

INT. MARRIOTT LOBBY – NIGHT

Maguire and Tidwell move through the brightly lit spectacle of the pre-draft lobby. Jerry works hard, introduces Tidwell around. The word 'Cush' appears often, everywhere. But Jerry uses his juice to get Tidwell noticed. They meet and greet many, passing even a Reebok ad being filmed. And Tidwell is a natural, polite and charming, as they move through the crowd. He blooms with the attention, as the music continues.

INT. MARRIOTT BAR – NIGHT

Tough red-headed beat reporter Patricia Logan watches Maguire and Tidwell from the opposite corner.

> PATRICIA
> Dennis, try not to laugh. Jerry Maguire brought *Rod Tidwell* to the draft . . .

INT. ARIZONA CARDINALS WAR ROOM (PHOENIX) – LATE DAY

Arizona general manager Dennis Wilburn, forty-eight, is on the phone here in the command center for the Arizona Cardinals.

> WILBURN
> Good, I hope he unloads him so I can buy a decent quarterback. Who's he talking to?

> PATRICIA
> Right now, Dallas.

> WILBURN
> They don't look interested, do they?

> PATRICIA
> Well, actually, yes . . .

INT. MARRIOTT ESCALATOR – NIGHT

Jerry and Tidwell rise triumphantly to the mezzanine level above the bright-white lobby. Maguire looks down at the scene. He breathes in the commotion. In another twelve hours, he will be at the very epicenter with Cushman.

> TIDWELL
> I came all this way *to walk the lobby*?

> JERRY
> Yeah. And it might have even worked, too.

> TIDWELL
> Let's do it again.

Down in the lobby, Jerry catches a glimpse of a familiar-looking agent.

93

It's Sugar. Tidwell continues looking at a commercial being filmed in the lobby.

TIDWELL
Lookit that, they're filming a commercial down there.
Nobody asked *me* to participate. I ain't getting no love from
Chevy. I ain't getting no love from Pepsi. I ain't getting no
love from the Energizer Bunny. Ain't getting no love from
Nike. Ain't getting no love from Reebok . . . Did I ever tell
you my Reebok story?

JERRY
I gotta get back to Cushman.

TIDWELL
Okay, I understand. I'll boil it down for ya. *Fuck Reebok.* All
they do is ignore me . . . Always have!

Jerry turns to Tidwell, finally focusing totally on him.

94

JERRY

Rod. You know what was great about you down there? For
about five minutes, you unloaded that rather large chip that
resides right there on your shoulder, and you know what?
You let people *in*, and you were brilliant. Take care. See you
tomorrow.

Jerry starts to exit, but Tidwell loves the attention.

TIDWELL

You're loving me now, aren't ya?

JERRY
(*exiting, moving*)
I'm not about love – I'm about 'showing you the money'.

TIDWELL

Good. I was just testing ya. But just you saying that? *Makes*
me love you.

JERRY

Get some sleep. See you tomorrow.

TIDWELL

Come on, man. It's New York City! Let's go out and find
some karaoke!

*Jerry exits, laughing as his beeper sounds and he looks at it. Hang on
Tidwell who now feels rather good about himself. He nods powerfully to
some passing Jets fans. They have no idea who he is.*

INT. CUSH'S SUITE – NIGHT

*Jerry enters Frank Cushman's suite on a rush of adrenalin. The room
overlooks Times Square. Matt, Keith and Cush's college girlfriend
Anne-Louise mill about the room service and free merchandise-filled
room, basking in the glow of the man of the moment. Cush, who holds a
guitar in his lap, wears the odd combo of a Nirvana T-shirt and an
NFL jacket. He signs for more room service and continues strumming
the only song he can play.*

CUSH
(*to hotel waiter*)
Hey, what size are you?

WAITER
Eleven.

CUSH
Why don't you grab a couple pairs of them new Reeboks by
the door –

Waiter spots a very tall stack of new Reeboks by the door.

WAITER
(*exiting*)
Dude, you're like a God.

CUSH
(*immediately*)
God, you're like a dude.

*The room breaks up. This is charisma, the future of the NFL. Cush
continues strumming. And now Jerry speaks, importantly.*

JERRY
Cush, Matt – we have a decision to make.

CUSH
'It's okay to eat fish, 'cause . . .'

JERRY
San Diego just came in with a last-minute scenario. It's
big.

CUSH
'. . . they don't have any feelings . . . '

MATT
Well, he's gotta go number one.

CUSH
'. . . Something in the way, yeah . . .

JERRY

He still goes number one, but San Diego wants to trade up
with Denver. They want him bad.

*Cush turns to his curiously ambivalent father, who walks to the window
and looks out at the big Jumbotron with Keith.*

MATT

What happened to Denver?

JERRY

Denver got very silent about a day ago. San Diego's got a
fever for Cush. This stuff tends to happen the night before a
draft. People get crazy. And San Diego, you should know, is
crazy to the tune of seven years for thirty. Signing bonus of
eight.

ANNE-LOUISE

Million?

*Suddenly, they all look at her. She flutters her hands, knowing she's
committed a* faux pas. *In the next room, the phone is ringing.*

MATT

But what happened to Denver?

KEITH

Should I unplug the phone?

CUSH

Reporters, Jerry. They been callin' all night. I feel like cat
food for a buncha hungry pussies.

JERRY

Just be friendly and say 'no comment'.

CUSH

Talking and saying nothing, man, is an art I have not
mastered.

*Something is off in the room, but Jerry picks up the ringing phone. He
offers a near-perfect imitation.*

JERRY

'This is Cush.'

All laugh.

INTERCUT WITH:

INT. BOB SUGAR'S HOTEL ROOM – NIGHT

Bob Sugar talks on his hotel phone.

> SUGAR
>
> It's Sugar. He must be there, right? Just sniff or something if he's there.
> (*as Jerry sniffs, panicked*)
> Alright, buddydude. Just remember. You're swimming with the big boys now. You let your dad do all the talking. I'm the one who got you the deal you needed. This is business, not friendship. Be strong. You're global now.

Sugar hangs up.

> JERRY
>
> 'No comment'.

Jerry hangs up. The room is laughing. His head is spinning.

> KEITH
>
> Hey, it's Cush on the big TV again!

> CUSH
>
> Hell, I'm already sick of me. I got 'Cushlash'.

Jerry sits across from Matt, reeling quietly.

> JERRY
>
> Look, before I get back to Denver. I think we should put something down on paper. Something that says, 'Hey, I'm with Jerry Maguire.'

> MATT
>
> Not right now, Jerry.

> JERRY
>
> Do I know everything there is to know here?
> (*silent beat*)
> You fellas aren't talking with Bob Sugar, are you?

MATT

Apparently, Denver wanted to deal with him instead of you.

JERRY

Said who? Sugar?

MATT

Hey, I'm learning as I go.

JERRY

So you empowered Bob Sugar to deal with Denver behind my back?

MATT

I'm sorry, I –

Jerry is full of crazy anger.

JERRY

I brought Denver to twenty million. Denver deals with me all the time. You listened to *Sugar*? You let that snake in the *door*.

Jerry touches the coffee table. Calms himself.

It's okay. You want Denver. I'll fix this up. You didn't sign anything with Sugar, right?

Silence.

KEITH
(blurts)

Mr Maguire, someday I'm gonna be a famous athlete and I'm gonna sign with you!

JERRY

Shut up!
(beat)
I'm sorry . . . sorry.

KEITH
(sympathy for Jerry)

S'cool.

99

JERRY

Now. Wait. You didn't actually sign with Sugar, did you? Tell me you didn't sign.
                              (*beat*)
Because I'm still sort of moved by your 'my word is stronger'n oak' thing –

MATT

We signed an hour ago. You were in the lobby with the black fella.

CUSH

I'm sorry, Jerry.

Silently, Jerry begins gathering his things. He takes a breath before he exits. Visible behind Maguire is Times Square in all its neon logo glory.

JERRY

Well. Okay. Of course. You're twenty years old, and I'm just another guy in a suit. It's all business. It didn't work out. You didn't buy my product, which is, unfortunately, *me*. But I'll be out there cheering for you. The door is always open!
                              (*breath, directly*)
But maybe this would have all worked, us being real human beings, coming through for each other, *really*, and now I'll never know. You'll never know. Weren't you curious?
                              (*they aren't*)
No. Okay, well, I'll be fine. And you'll be fine. And Keith, I hope you do call me.

Flushed and embarrassed, he exits. We hang a beat on the silent Cushman hotel living room, as Cush begins to strum again.

INT. HOTEL HALLWAY – NIGHT

Maguire moves swiftly down the hallway, whips past us.

Jerry exits elevator dazed, at full trot. He is looking for Avery. Beat reporter Patricia Logan reappears.

PATRICIA LOGAN

Jerry, is it true that Tidwell's had three concussions?

> JERRY

I'm sorry . . . excuse me . . .

INT. BALLROOM – NIGHT

Jerry enters the grand ballroom, looking for Avery. NFL reps and endorsement placards in evidence everywhere. Jerry spots Avery across the empty ballroom, moving fast, passing out media packets on the empty tables.

INT. ADJACENT BUFFET ROOM – NIGHT

> AVERY

I just heard.

> JERRY

What do I do? How do I spin this?

> AVERY

Oh, honey. It's *spun*.

> JERRY

What did I do to *you*?

She is furious with his question. Doesn't he know?

> AVERY

It's all about you, isn't it? Soothe *me*, save *me*, love *me* –

> JERRY

Could you just stop moving?

> AVERY

I have to finish my job –

> JERRY

Everything's on the fucking run! Everything –

She stops. Walks to him, framed by a bank of TV monitors.

> AVERY

Jerry. You and I are salespeople. We *sell* –

> JERRY

Look, I don't want a –

AVERY

It's not 'love me'. It's not 'trust my handshake'. It's *make the sale*. Get it *signed*. There shouldn't be 'confusion' about *that*.

JERRY

Go ahead. Jump right on into my nightmare. The water's warm.

AVERY

So honesty is outlawed here, I can't be honest?

JERRY

Tell you what – I'd prefer loyalty.

AVERY

What was our deal when we first got together? Brutal truth, remember?

JERRY

I think you added the 'brutal'.

She stops, slaps down another media packet. Blows a troublesome piece of hair out of her face.

AVERY

Jerry, there is a 'sensitivity' thing that some people have. I don't have it. I don't cry at movies. I don't gush over babies. I don't start celebrating Christmas five months early, and I don't tell a man who just screwed up *both* of our lives – 'Oh, poor baby.' That's me. For better or worse. But I do love you.

Jerry looks at his fiancée. Standing here, watching Avery coldly clasping her media packs to her chest, she looks different to him.

JERRY

Avery –

She moves fast to avoid what's coming.

AVERY

Don't say it. We've both ragged out right now.

JERRY

– stop –

She turns. They face off. They are quickly interrupted by large, talk show-voiced Curtis Weintraub, thirty-seven.

> CURTIS WEINTRAUB
>
> Hey! Curtis Weintraub from the *Sports Popper*! Haven't seen you two since the Six Flags Charity Rock 'n' Sock Cuervo Gold Budfest! Hello!

Curtis gets a whiff of what he walked into.

> *(exiting quickly)*
>
> Goodbye!

> AVERY
>
> I'm warning you. Don't say it. You won't have another chance.

> JERRY
>
> Listen to me!

> AVERY
>
> No.

> JERRY
>
> It's over –

> AVERY
> *(she takes off again)*
>
> Didn't hear it.

> JERRY
>
> There is something missing here.

> AVERY
>
> You've never been alone and you *can't* be alone –

> JERRY
>
> Listen to me, it's *over*.

She can barely believe it. She blinks.

> AVERY
>
> No one has ever dumped me.

> JERRY
>
> I'm not trying to make history.

AVERY

I did the twenty-three-hour nose-route to the top of El
Capitan in *eighteen hours and twenty-three minutes*. I can make
this work.

JERRY
(*it slips out*)

No.

From somewhere, the small voice of her vulnerability.

AVERY

Oh, Jerry.

JERRY
(*steps closer*)

You know I didn't ever want to hurt you.

*She gets an odd look, shaking her head. Starts to step away, then thinks
better of it. She wallops him in the face with the back of her hand. Jerry
stands like a woozy boxer. She hits him again with a fist, then again in
the chest. He sinks to the floor, sagging backwards. She straddles him,
leans in close.*

AVERY

I won't let you hurt me, Jerry. I'm too strong for you. *Loser.*

EXT. TIMES SQUARE – NEXT DAY

*Jerry exits in sunglasses, Tidwell close behind. Both carry their hang-up
bags. Jerry attempts to hail a cab.*

TIDWELL

Too bad about Cushman.

JERRY

Taxi!

TIDWELL

You love me *now*, don't you?

JERRY

Very much. *Taxi!*

Tidwell watches his agitated agent.

TIDWELL

Is it my imagination, or did we *arrive* here in a limo?

Jerry shoots a look at Tidwell, continues trying to hail a cab.

REPORTER #1

Is it San Diego or Denver, Jerry?

JERRY

I don't give a shit!!

(*as cabs pass*)

Taxi!

ON TV MONITOR – ROY FIRESTONE

is leaning forward, expressively, talking with a weepy athlete.

INT. RED CARPET LOUNGE – AFTERNOON

Tidwell watches next to Jerry, as they wait for the flight. Jerry nurses a stiff drink.

TIDWELL

Everybody on this show cries now.

JERRY

Rod –

TIDWELL

(*off TV*)

You feel bad you tested positive? Quit doing blow! You feel bad about your baby girl? Why did you leave the mother?

JERRY

What are you doing with me, Rod?

TIDWELL

Huh?

JERRY

Don't you even see – I'm finished. I'm fucked. Twenty-four hours ago, I was *hot*. Now . . . I'm a cautionary tale!

Tidwell looks at Jerry, impassive.

See this jacket I'm wearing? You like it? I don't really need it, because I'm *cloaked in failure*. I lost the *number one draft* pick the night before the draft. They will teach my story to other agents on 'do not do this' day in agent school. Why? Let's recap. Because a hockey player's kid made me feel like a superficial jerk, I had two slices of bad pizza, went to bed, grew a conscience and wrote a twenty-five-page *Manifesto of Doom*!

TIDWELL

Well, boo-fucking-hoo.

JERRY

The least you could do is nod and act sympathetic –

TIDWELL
(*shaking head*)

No.

JERRY

It's a quality that might come in handy for a commercial sometime.

TIDWELL

You are not allowed to act this way.

JERRY

Why not?

INT. AIRPLANE – AFTERNOON (LATER)

They sit together. Jerry holds another drink.

TIDWELL

Man, I got a shelf-life of ten years, tops! My next contract's gotta bring me the dollars that'll last me and mine a very long time. I'm out of this sport in five years. What's my family gonna live on? What you get me. So I don't want to hear about ya shit, your 'nya nya nya'.

JERRY
(*ruefully, to attendant*)

Another drink, please.

106

TIDWELL

Anybody else would have left you by now, but I'm sticking with you. I said I would. And if I got to ride your ass like Zorro, you're gonna *show me the money.*

JERRY
(*the hell that never ends*)

Oh, my God.

He looks straight ahead, at the airphone in front of him.

EXT. PORCH – NIGHT

Dorothy finds Laurel on their small porch.

DOROTHY

He's coming over.

LAUREL

Tonight?

DOROTHY

He just lost his best client. He called from the plane. I invited the guy over.

LAUREL

Dotty – this is not 'guy'. This is a 'syndrome'. It's called Early Midlife, About-To-Marry, Hanging Onto-the-Bottom-Rung, Dear-God-Don't-Let-Me-Be-Alone, I'll-Call-My-Newly-Long-Shuffering-Assistant-Without-Medical-For-Company Syndrome. And if, knowing all that, you still allow him to come over, more power to you.

DOROTHY

Honey, he's *engaged.* And for the first time in my professional life, I'm a part of something I believe in.

Dorothy exits. Laurel shakes her head, calls to next room.

LAUREL

Okay, but he better not be good-looking!

107

INT. RAY'S BEDROOM – NIGHT

Dorothy puts Ray to bed.

> DOROTHY
> Night, buddy. This is my favorite part of your head.

She kisses the corner of his forehead, rising up into the mirror. She checks her look, in spite of herself. Her late husband's photo is visible over Ray's head. Music.

INT. CAB – NIGHT (LATER)

Jerry in back of a cab, three drinks later, wearing sunglasses.

> JERRY
> Okay, turn here! Sharp right turn. 8831–3/4 Waterloo.

The cab turns on to a very small street. Down the street, another pair of headlights. Jerry's cab refuses to give in, in fact he floors it. Same with the oncoming car.

> Yes, good, floor it, kill us!!

EXT. DOROTHY'S FRONT PORCH – NIGHT

Door opens to reveal Jerry Maguire with bags, disheveled hair and sunglasses.

> JERRY
> I'm Jerry Maguire.

> LAUREL
> *(super pleasant)*
> You seem just the way I pictured you. I'm her disapproving sister Laurel.

> JERRY
> Honesty. *Thank you.*

INT. LIVING ROOM – NIGHT – CONTINUOUS ACTION

Dorothy enters, expertly casual.

DOROTHY

Hey, you.

JERRY

Hi. Thanks for inviting me over. Where's the little guy?

DOROTHY

He's asleep. Watch out for that lamp.

JERRY

I'm glad you're home. That 'alone' thing is . . . not my speciality . . .

He ducks the lamp, barely. Laurel exits through his shot, miming 'drinking' behind his back. Jerry takes off his glasses, revealing a welt and a cut below his eye.

DOROTHY

Oh, my God.

JERRY

Yeah. That too. I broke up with Avery.

DOROTHY
(entire body chemistry shifts)

Too bad.

JERRY

Better now than later. We'll still be friends. I'm dying here.

DOROTHY

Jesus, it's a real *gash*, isn't it?

JERRY

And just think if I got her the ring she *really* wanted.

Dorothy laughs.

DOROTHY

Sorry. Let me see, have a seat. I'll get you some aloe vera for that cut too.

JERRY

Do you have something to drink?

DOROTHY

Sure –

She is about to exit to the kitchen, when Jerry begins to unburden.

JERRY

My brother works for NASA. He is currently growing algae in
space that will one day feed the world.

She waits politely for Jerry to finish searching for his point.

I was supposed to be the successful one. But I don't want to
get into this. And yet! My family. I grew up with repression as
a . . . a religion – you don't bitch. No moaning! Head down.
Do it, whatever 'it' may be. My dad . . . he worked for the
United Way for thirty-eight years! You know what he said
when he retired? He said, 'I wish they'd given me a more
comfortable chair.' Thirty-eight years he sat in it! Do you
know what I'm saying, Dorothy? Repression as a *religion*. I'm
almost as old as his chair.

DOROTHY

Beer okay?

JERRY

Yeah, thanks. You're so easy to talk with.

INT. KITCHEN

Dorothy goes for the refrigerator.

LAUREL

I heard.

DOROTHY

No kidding. I looked over and saw the shadow of two *curious
shoes* in the doorway of the kitchen.

LAUREL

This guy would go home with a gardening tool right now if it
showed interest.
                    (*off Dorothy's look*)
Wait. Use the frosted glasses.

                    DOROTHY
                    (*surprised*)
Thank you.

                    LAUREL
Look, here's some of that chicken with salsa too, I warmed it
up –

                    DOROTHY
That's the girl I love.

                    LAUREL
But you just gotta hear me out on one thing. You're very
responsible with Ray and you know it's not right for a little
boy to hear some strange man's voice in the house.

                    DOROTHY
As opposed to ten angry women?

*Dorothy turns quickly and the beer, sisters and chicken collide in the
small kitchen. Dorothy deftly catches the food in her T-shirt, and dumps
it back on to the plate. But her shirt is now stained. She starts to
implode quietly, and Laurel takes command. They know each other
well.*

                    LAUREL
Come on, let's get you another top.

They exit to nearby laundry room.

EXT. HOUSE – WINDOW OUTSIDE LAUNDRY ROOM – NIGHT

*Camera starts to move around the house, from this window showing the
two sisters in the laundry room, to the living room where Jerry sits alone.
We see Ray wander into the room and stare at Jerry.*

INT. LIVING ROOM – NIGHT

Jerry, playing with a kaleidoscope, looks up to see Ray.

                    RAY
Hi.

                    III

Hi, Ray.

INT. LAUNDRY ROOM – SAME TIME

LAUREL

All I'm saying. You don't have the luxury of falling for some drowning man. Be practical. Now. Which top?

She holds up two tops. One is sexier with a plunging neckline. The other is striped, cute, functional.

DOROTHY

Okay, you want to talk about practical? Let's talk about my wonderful life. Do you know what most other women my age are doing right now? They are partying in clubs, trying to act stupid, trying to get a man, trying to keep a man . . . not me. I'm trying to *raise* a man.

She grabs the sexier top, and puts in on.

I've got a twenty-four-hour-a-day reminder of Roger, for the rest of my life. I have had three lovers in four years, all boring, all achingly self-sufficient, all friends of yours, I might add, and all of them running a distant second to a warm bath. Look at me, Laurel, look at me. I'm the oldest twenty-six-year-old in the world! How do I look?

LAUREL

Good.

DOROTHY

Thanks.

INT. LIVING ROOM – NIGHT

Jerry and Ray play tug with a piece of rope.

RAY

And then my dad died and my mom took me to the zoo and I love the zoo. Do you hate the zoo or do you love the zoo?

JERRY

Wait. I want to tell you more about *my* dad.

RAY

Let's go the zoo.

JERRY

Okay. I've been hogging it. You're right. All my life I've been trying to talk, really talk, and no one wants to listen. You know that feeling?

Ray nods vigorously.

RAY

Let's go right now. Let's go to the zoo.

JERRY

Aw, the fucking thing . . . I mean, the zoo is closed.

RAY

You said 'fuck'!

JERRY

Yeah, I know. I did.

Ray loves this guy. He pats Jerry's knee.

RAY

I won't tell.

JERRY

We'll go to the zoo sometime. Okay? I think I might have some time on my hands.

RAY

I don't see any.

JERRY
(*points respectfully*)

Funny.

Jerry smiles. He likes this kid. What is this oddly satisfying feeling? His cellular phone rings.

JERRY

Jerry Maguire.

TIDWELL BATHROOM – NIGHT

Rod Tidwell sits in a bathtub with Advertising Age *and a cellular. A small TV on corner of tub. Tyson plays in the foreground.*

> TIDWELL
> You're dreaming about me, baby? Because I want my agent thinking about me *all the time*. That's when the big dollars are gonna flow, when my face is in your head, *constantly* . . .

INT. DOROTHY'S LIVING ROOM – NIGHT

Wearily, Maguire shakes his head. He can take no more of Tidwell. He hands the phone to Ray, who listens to Tidwell's creed, entertained.

> JERRY
> (*to himself*)
> He doesn't even know he's probably too small for the NFL.

> RAY
> (*like a shot*)
> You're too small for the NFL.

Immediately panicked, Jerry looks at Ray. Ray looks at Jerry. Ray throws the phone down, and it disconnects.

INT. TIDWELL BATHROOM – NIGHT

Tidwell sits silent in the bathtub. First time we've seen him silenced.

INT. DOROTHY'S LIVING ROOM – NIGHT

Laughing at Jerry's face, Ray now hears his mother approaching.

> RAY
> Igagotobed.

Camera swings to the kitchen door, where Dorothy emerges with tray.

> DOROTHY
> Drinks. Food. Plus, I called you a cab.

Jerry looks up, confused and somehow entertained by the swirling madness around him.

JERRY

Good idea. Thank you.

DOROTHY

And we should keep our voices down a little. I have a little
boy asleep.

JERRY

Right. Of course.

DOROTHY

So. Our company.

*Jerry takes a swig of beer. Then coughs a little, then stands, woozy but
loose, looking around the small house of this single mother and sister. He
feels a powerful need to announce:*

JERRY

Okay. Lil' speech before I go. Do. Not. Worry. About. Your.
Job.

(*beat*)

Our company is in good shape. You and your son . . . *we* . . .
are just fine. You still have a job. I want you to feel confident!
In. Me. And I have a problem with people who talk about
themselves in the third person, but let me tell you *something*
about Jerry Maguire.

*His confidence nicely fueled, Jerry reaches for a fireplace poker. He
begins to joust with an imaginary opponent.*

Come after me and *you will lose*. I am a survivor! Do not
underestimate Jerry Maguire! I've got wits! I've got the
instincts of a panther!

(*joust*)

I've got Dorothy Boyd on my side!

DOROTHY

Don't worry about me. I can get jobs –

JERRY

We will be fine!

DOROTHY

– especially one like this.

115

JERRY

And I am . . .

She takes the fireplace poker from him. He becomes very aware of himself. Acting out in a virtual stranger's small but comfortable living room.

. . . I am *drunk.*

He collapses on to the sofa, embarrassed. Dorothy scoots closer in an adjacent chair. She breaks the personal barrier, carefully touching his wound with the wet tip of the aloe vera plant.

DOROTHY

Truth?

JERRY

Sure.

DOROTHY

Sure, I care about the job. Of course. But mostly . . .
  (*very honest*)
. . . I want to be inspired.

There is something inspiring about the way she says the word 'inspired'.

JERRY

Me, too.

DOROTHY

What you wrote inspired me.

He is catching a scent of that most ancient elixir. A woman's affection. Their heads inch closer together.

I'm working with you because of that memo . . .

JERRY

. . . Mission . . . Statement . . .

They kiss. It turns rather passionate. She places a cool hand on his cheek. He places a hand on her breast. The taxi beeps outside. She pulls away. Both regard the hand on her breast.

Well.

JERRY

Sorry about this hand.
                    (*he rises unsteadily*)
You know that feeling – you're not completely embarrassed
yet, but you *glimpse* tomorrow's embarrassment?

DOROTHY

Don't worry about it, boss.

JERRY

Oh, shit. You said 'boss'.

DOROTHY

Yeah, I did.

JERRY

Now I feel like Clarence Thomas.

DOROTHY

No. No, don't feel like Clarence Thomas.

JERRY

No, I do. I feel like Clarence Thomas.
                    (*the worst day ever*)
I'm like . . . harassing you . . . *right now*.

DOROTHY

I may not sue.

He laughs a little. Unsure what more to say, Jerry rubs his face.

JERRY

Well, good evening.

DOROTHY

Good evening.

*He exits. Stumbling slightly on the first step, leading down from the
front porch, he recovers with style.*

JERRY

We'll be okay. And I'm going to take my . . . one client and
we're gonna go all the way.

(*loving the dark humor*)
Hey. I'm *back*.

Dorothy watches him exit. She regards the poker still in her hand.
Laurel watches her conflicted, slightly lovesick sister.

INT. CAB – NIGHT

Jerry in the back of the cab. He turns for a moment, looking back at the
warm house he's just left. Something is scratching at his soul, trying to
get in. Music continues. He was strangely comfortable there, as the
house disappears from his view. He looks out at the neighborhood, as if
it were a museum of domesticity.

JERRY
All those yellow windows . . . all those lives . . . Great . . .

FADE TO:

EXT. TEMPE PRACTICE AREA/WORKOUT – DAY

Rod Tidwell races to catch up to a wobbly, overthrown pass. He snags it
out of the air, and moves gracefully downfield. He turns back to shout
at the quarterback for the bad pass ('You're hanging me out to dry,
man'), and slams into a padded post. Dennis Wilburn crosses in front of
Maguire, giving him a look.

JERRY
We gotta talk about his contract, Dennis.

WILBURN
Meet me at eight at the Crocodile.

INT. CROCODILE STEAK HOUSE – NIGHT

Maguire waits. And waits. And looks at his watch. And waits.

EXT. WILBURN'S HOME – SUNRISE

Dennis Wilburn exits his home in a gated area of Phoenix. He is
wearing golf attire, carries clubs. Birds are chirping. Maguire appears
from behind some shrubbery.

JERRY

Morning, Dennis.

WILBURN

Morning, Jerry.

*Wilburn looks busted, but doesn't apologize. He goes about taking the
targa-top off his sports car. Maguire helps.*

JERRY

Ten million for four years.

WILBURN
(*scoffing noises*)

It's early. You're still dreaming.

JERRY

Ten for four is what's fair.

*Wilburn gives Jerry a look, they continue struggling with the top of the
car. Maguire notes the simple fact that Wilburn will never care as much
about a player as he does about this car.*

Then trade him or let me take him to Dallas.

WILBURN

Dallas? *Please –*

JERRY

Dennis, this guy respects you. He loves *you*. You're like a
father figure to him.

WILBURN

Then, how about if I pay him 300 for two years, and *hug* him a
lot.

JERRY
(*steely*)

Listen, you're in a very precarious position. If I were you, and
by the way we're all sad your dad passed away, but I'd be
worried about my own job now. I'd want to win. I wouldn't
insult the agent who brought you some of your best players.
And, I wouldn't let my best receiver get away. Fax me your
best offer this week. Good morning.

INT. LOCKER ROOM SHOWER AREA – DAY

Jerry stands in the locker room. Off-screen we hear a shower.

> JERRY
>
> I started talking with Dennis Wilburn about your renegotiation.

Tidwell emerges naked, dripping wet, pissed.

> TIDWELL
>
> 'Talking?'
>
> > (*beat*)
>
> Michael Irvin! Jerry Rice! Chris Carter! I *smoke* all these fools, and yet they're making the big sweet dollars. They're making the –
>
> > (*fingers word like silk*)
>
> – the kwan. And you're, talking!

> JERRY
>
> 'Kwan'? That's your word?

> TIDWELL
>
> Yeah. Some people have the coin, but they'll never have the kwan. It means love, respect, community . . . and the dollars, too. The package. The *kwan*.

> JERRY
>
> Great word. Towel?

> TIDWELL
>
> No, I air-dry.

> JERRY
>
> Rod, I say this with great respect, but those players you mentioned are marquee players and –

> TIDWELL
>
> > (*phone beeps*)
>
> Is that your porty or mine?

> JERRY
>
> You.

Tidwell rummages in his bag. Finds one of two porties and answers the one with a Polaroid of Marcee taped to it.

> **TIDWELL**
> Hi, baby. Yeah, I'm just breakin' in the new agent. He says I'm not marquee. I *know* . . . I know . . .

Tidwell holds up the phone so Jerry can hear the sound of Marcee going off.

> My wife is upset with you.

INT. LOCKER ROOM MIRROR – DAY

The conversation continues as the still-naked Tidwell fixes his hair in the mirror. Jerry is earnest, passionate.

> **JERRY**
> Here's what I'm saying. This is a renegotiation. We want more from them, so let's give them more. Let's show them your *pure joy* of the game, let's bury the Attitude a little, let's show them –

> **TIDWELL**
> (*irritated*)
> You're telling me to dance.

> **JERRY**
> No, I'm saying to be –

He mimes a dainty little showboat touchdown dance.

> **TIDWELL**
> (*little voice*)
> 'Love me love me love me . . . put me on TV. Hello, white America!'
> (*pissed*)
> That's the iconography of *racism*, man!

Marcee's voice emerges from Tidwell's cellular, near the mirror.

> **MARCEE**
> (*voice-over*)
> I agree with everything he just said.

121

JERRY

Rod, *Marcee*, I'm not a racist. I'm telling you to be the best
version of you, to get back to the guy who first started playing
this game. Way back when you were a kid. It wasn't just
about the money, was it?

Tidwell gives him a look. Money was always a factor.

TIDWELL

Do your job, man, don't tell me to dance.

JERRY

Fine.

He begins gathering his things.

TIDWELL

I'm an *athlete*, not an entertainer. These are the ABCs of *me*.
Get it? *I don't dance.* And I *don't* start pre-season without a
contract.

Jerry rubs face.

What's wrong.

JERRY

Forget it. Forget it.

TIDWELL

No, tell me.

JERRY

I'm out here for you! You don't *know* what it's like to be *me*
out here for *you*. It is an up-at-dawn pride-swallowing siege
that I will *never fully tell you about*! Okay?! Help me help you
help me help you.

TIDWELL

You're hanging by a very thin thread, dude. And I dig that
about you.

Jerry has had enough for one day.

JERRY
(*loopy, punch-drunk*)
Hey. I'm happy to entertain you! I'll see you in LA!

Tidwell watches his agent lurch off, muttering and swaying.

TIDWELL
See, man, that's the difference between us. You think we're
fighting, I think we're finally talking!

INT. LAX AIRPORT – DAY

*Jerry moves slowly through crowded airport, preoccupied. The job
definitely used to be easier.*

INT. JERRY'S HOME OFFICE – DAY (LATER)

*Jerry enters, carrying bag, weary. Dorothy greets him. They are stuck in
his small condo, and the scent of their previous encounter is still in the
air. She hands him a list of his calls.*

DOROTHY
Dennis Wilburn called from Arizona to say he's faxing in the
new Tidwell offer on Thursday morning. We could sure use
that commission. I did some work on your finances . . .

She hands him a company report she's done. He takes a quick look.

JERRY
I sunk most of what I had into this condo, which devalued,
and –

DOROTHY
You don't have to explain.

JERRY
Look, the other night, I want to apologize.

DOROTHY
(*can't read him*)
Yeah, what happened there.

JERRY
We're two people working together and we can't have an
atmosphere.

123

DOROTHY

I'm relieved you said that.

JERRY

I mean, the other night was . . . you know, lonely . . . I felt
you understood something, what I was trying to say.

DOROTHY

What were you trying to say?

JERRY

I don't know. I was . . . I remember the better points of the
evening, I remember *you*, and your son.
(*beat*)
But we have a company here to think about. I won't ever take
advantage of you in that way again.

DOROTHY
(*evenly*)

Oh, good.

JERRY

You walked out on a job for me, and look how I repay you –

DOROTHY
(*a look*)

Exactly because I know this is a time when you need to be
alone with your thoughts. Think about everything that's gone
wrong, how to fix it, and just be . . . alone, alone, alone.

Dorothy in the background of the shot, watching his reaction.

JERRY

You want to go out to dinner?

INT. DOROTHY'S LIVING ROOM – NIGHT

*Dorothy looks for a jacket as Laurel helms the divorced women's group
in the living room. Jan speaks through her whistly braces, gesturing
with a too-full glass of red wine.*

JAN

I broke up with the cowboy. And now he's stalking me . . .

ALICE

What's the current definition of stalking?

WOMAN #1

Coming over uninvited.

JAN
(*thoughtful*)

So Romeo under the trellis . . . was a stalker.

WOMAN #1

Exactly.

Dorothy finds the jacket.

INT. HALLWAY – NIGHT

Dorothy stops in the hallway to see that Jerry has arrived at the kitchen door.

She watches unseen as Maguire shakes hands with Chad and is hit suddenly by a flying hug from Ray. Laurel nods to Jerry, who gives the kid an athletic bag, which is filled with state-of-the-art promotional athletic wear, etc. Then he gives him an energy bar.

LAUREL

See, now, that's not a good idea.

Jerry gives Laurel a hat. She looks at it, smiles, doesn't put it on.

INT. KITCHEN – NIGHT

Jerry plays with the kid, as Dorothy enters.

DOROTHY

Hey, looks like you've got a fan.

JERRY
(*outdressed*)

Wow. That's more than a dress. That's an Audrey Hepburn movie.

DOROTHY

Yeah – guess I got revved up at the idea of an evening among adults – no offense, buster.

LAUREL

Jerry, did you meet Chad?

JERRY

Yeah, I did – am I dressed okay? I guess I didn't realize we
were . . .

*He doesn't finish the words 'going out on a date'. He watches, amused,
at the small circus that swirls around this kitchen.*

DOROTHY

Don't let him stay up too late.

CHAD
(*grandly*)

Hey, man, tonight I'm going to teach Ray about jazz.

DOROTHY

Good, that'll put him to sleep early. No offense.

*Three women from the women's group enter the kitchen, still continuing
a conversation from the other room.*

CHAD

You know, you people have a jazz problem in this house.

RAY

I wanna go, too.

*Laurel gives Ray a look. Ray backs down, as Jerry hears snatches of the
women's group going full blast in the living room.*

DOROTHY

We'll see you soon, honey. Bye.

JERRY

Bye, you guys.

*Ray extends his arms, he wants a hug. Jerry bends down awkwardly to
give him one, and Ray plants a kiss on Jerry's cheek. All are surprised,
especially Jerry.* PUSH IN *on Dorothy. She is struck and moved.*

INT. KITCHEN – NIGHT

Laurel looks out the window, watches her sister exiting. She is equal parts jealous and protective. She spots keys on counter. She grabs them and runs out to catch her sister on the lawn.

EXT. DOROTHY'S HOUSE – NIGHT

Jerry and Dorothy exit through the many cars. The sound of the women's group is heard in the warmly glowing house behind them.

> LAUREL
Hey!

Jerry moves ahead, Dorothy to talk with Laurel privately.

Forgot your keys –

> DOROTHY
> (*quietly*)
That's the first time I ever saw him kiss a man, like a dad, wasn't that just . . . thrilling?
> (*eyes tear up*)
I mean, he must have been needing that.

> LAUREL
No no. Don't cry at the *beginning* of the date. Cry at the end, like I do.

> DOROTHY
> (*laughing, wiping tear*)
Oh, knock it off!

> LAUREL
> (*can't help it*)
And don't be a shoulder for him to cry on either.

We stay with Laurel as she watches her sister exit.

Oh dear.

Music continues. Lit by streetlight, Dorothy runs like a young girl, across the lawns of this car-filled neighborhood, slapping away the leaves of a tree, running to Jerry down the street.

INT. ANTONIO'S RESTAURANT – NIGHT

Jerry and Dorothy sit at the table of this Mexican restaurant. In the background, Mariachis play.

> JERRY
>
> It was laziness, my whole break-up with Avery. You know that thing you say, 'It's nobody's fault.' It's one of the great lies, right? Someone is always to blame – if you go for it, go for it like you do a job, work at it –

> DOROTHY
>
> Maybe love shouldn't be such hard work.

> JERRY
>
> I know, but –

Mariachis approach the table.

> HEAD MARIACHI
>
> A song for the lovers?

JERRY/DOROTHY
(*too quickly*)
No. No thanks.

DOROTHY
We work together.

Jerry slips the guy a few bucks to go away. They do so, reluctantly.

JERRY
See, you *choose*. If you fall for someone, if you make a
commitment, you should make it work. It's only when
'options' entered the picture that things got bad. I'm speaking
historically now. It's a modern day concept, neuroticism –
how do I *feeeeeel?* – I think the only good thing to come from
this period in history is probably the movie *Annie Hall.*

DOROTHY
(*evenly*)
Maybe you should call her.

JERRY
No no no. I just underestimated her . . .
(*touches wound*)
. . . her temper, I guess. Why are we even talking about this?

A Flower Girl approaches the table with an armful of roses.

FLOWER GIRL
A rose for the lady.

JERRY
You want a –

DOROTHY
(*scoffs*)
No. No way.

Jerry gives her few bucks, she exits.

Yeah. It wasn't like my marriage to Roger was so great, even
before –
(*stops herself*)
Jerry?

130

JERRY

What?

DOROTHY
(*simply*)
Let's not tell our sad stories.

Jerry laughs to himself. He admires her directness.

We're young, we're semi-successful. Life is good. Right?

He points at her. Yes. She exits.

INT. BATHROOM – NIGHT (MINUTES LATER)

Dorothy on the phone outside the bathroom.

DOROTHY
No. Now . . . come on . . . No, they *sting* . . . Let Chad catch
the bee in the glass. He won't hurt it. Aw, buddy, you got
such a good heart. I love you, I'll be home soon. Can't wait to
see you.

EXT. BATHROOM

*She exits the bathroom and stops at the sight of what is happening at
the table. Jerry, hand on face, is embarrassingly being serenaded by the
Mariachis, who now play a mournful 'Tears in Heaven'. She smiles at
the image, in fact the poetry charms her. Dorothy moves forward,
grinning, fishes some bucks out of her pocket, and sends the Mariachis
in another direction.*

DOROTHY
Come on, let's take a walk.

INT. DOROTHY'S PORCH – NIGHT

*Music feathers into sounds of the night. A bug buzzing from the nearby
light, Jerry swats it away.*

JERRY
Well – this would be good night.

131

DOROTHY

Good night.

JERRY

I'll see you tomorrow.

On impulse, she grabs him and pulls him close. Kisses him. It's a good one.

DOROTHY

Good night.

JERRY

Good night.

But they don't move. He pulls her closer by her straps. They break. She holds them up, nervous now. His lips travel down. He kisses her upper chest. She sighs deeply, she's missed this feeling. Jerry rises to kiss her lips again, tying her straps back on. Her expression says there is a decision to make. She concentrates on the Styrofoam container she's brought back from the restaurant.

DOROTHY
(*breath*)

I think you should not come in, or come in depending on how you feel.

JERRY

Same to you.

DOROTHY

No. I have to go in. I live here.

JERRY

Right. I'll come in.

DOROTHY

Okay. Wait here a second.
(*beat, then*)
Do we really want to do this?

JERRY
(*half unsure*)

Oh hell, yes.

132

INT. LIVING ROOM – NIGHT

Dorothy enters to find Chad watching TV. The house is now quiet, the remains of the divorced women's group is still evidence.

> DOROTHY
>
> He's asleep, right?

> CHAD
>
> Yeah, how'd it go?

> DOROTHY
>
> Still going.

Chad raises his eyebrows.

> Shhh.

EXT. PORCH – NIGHT

Jerry on the porch, as Chad exits.

> CHAD
>
> Treat her right, man. She's . . .

> JERRY
> (*self-conscious*)
>
> Yeah . . . well . . .

> CHAD
>
> She's great. And I know this is a little awkward, but I want you to use this.

Chad rummages in bag for a moment. Jerry is somewhat horrified at what Chad might be giving him. Out comes a cassette.

> (*intense*)
>
> This . . . is Miles Davis and John Coltrane. Stockholm. 1960 . . . Two masters of freedom, playing in a time before their art was corrupted by a zillion cocktail lounge performers who destroyed the legacy of the only American art form – *Jazz*.

Jerry takes the tape, as the front door squeaks open. Dorothy shoos Chad away, quietly leads Jerry inside.

INT. BEDROOM – NIGHT

Fierce, elegant, driving jazz. *Dorothy and Jerry making out on bed.
Getting hotter. The music gets wilder. Finally it is impossible to ignore,
and Jerry collapses backwards on the bed laughing. She is left frozen,
her arms open but he is gone.*

> DOROTHY
> What is this *music?*

*They both crack up, and she kisses him as the music plays. He looks
at her. She turns away, then back again, he's still looking at her.
It's a powerful moment for her. Laughter continues, the music is
ridiculous. (Their sex is very different from the let's-be-intense sex
with Avery.)*

INT. KITCHEN – NIGHT (SAME TIME)

*Laurel, just home from work in her nurse's uniform, has a late-night
joint and carefully blows the smoke out the window. She helps herself to
the appetizers in the Styrofoam container. Listening to the laughter.*

INT. DOROTHY'S BEDROOM – NIGHT

CLOSER SHOT, *still kissing. Hands exploring each other's bodies.*

> DOROTHY
> I can't stop my brain.

> JERRY
> I can't stop my hands.

> DOROTHY
> Well, we're a good match, I guess.

> JERRY
> Right . . . right . . .

> DOROTHY
> A little to the left would be good, too.
> (*as they kiss*)
> I was worried you can't afford me and now I don't care . . . I
> mean, I do have an outstanding job offer in San Diego, with
> the Chargers. And maybe I should take that offer because

you're . . . you're a little broke right now. I was looking for an opportunity to bring this up, and –

He silences her with another kiss.

> JERRY
>
> You're a great accountant.

> DOROTHY
>
> Why?

> JERRY
>
> They never pick the right time to tell you the bad news, but you sure do.

> DOROTHY
>
> Well, thanks.

> JERRY
>
> Stop your brain. We're going to be fine.

They kiss.

> DOROTHY
>
> You're not going to yell, are you? These walls are really thin.

He mimes yelling, and she laughs.

> JERRY
>
> You know what? I'm beginning to like jazz.

DISSOLVE TO:

INT. DOROTHY'S BEDROOM – MORNING

Clock radio clicks on. It's still dark. Only the glow of the digital lamp. Jerry alone in bed. He gets up, coughs, jumps to his feet and looks for his pants.

> JERRY
> (*to himself; rueful*)
> Wonderful. You really needed to do this . . .

He maneuvers through a strange bedroom, steps on strange toys.

INT. KITCHEN – MORNING

Dorothy and Laurel in the kitchen, waiting for the coffee.

DOROTHY
I'm getting him up, don't worry! Ray will never see his
mother's raging physical needs.

LAUREL
First you gotta tell me something.

DOROTHY
No –

INT. HALLWAY – MORNING

Jerry moving down the hallway, hears voices.

INT. KITCHEN – CUTTING BACK AND FORTH – MORNING

LAUREL
Because I'm worried that you're putting your faith in this guy
who, because of the way things are going, may not have an
emotional marble in his head.

DOROTHY
Please, if I start talking –

LAUREL
Guys are just different people when they're hanging on to the
bottom rung.

ON JERRY – *listening.*

DOROTHY
. . . so what am I, for taking the opportunity, Laurel? Maybe I
am taking advantage. Am I a bad person? All I know is that I
found someone who was charming and popular and not-so-
nice to me – and he died. Okay? So why should I let this guy
go, when everything in my body says This One is *the* One.

LAUREL
Easy, hon, I was just looking for fun details –

DOROTHY

Oh, well, why didn't you say so? And oh, I don't know if you're interested in this detail, but I was just about to tell you that I love him. I love him, and I don't care what you think. I love him for the guy he wants to be, and I love him for the guy he almost is. I love him.

ON JERRY

He is rubbing his face.

RAY
(*surprising all parties*)

Hi, Jerry!

Dorothy leans into the hallway now, sees Jerry standing there, well within earshot. As Ray happily enters.

DOROTHY

Oh, God.

JERRY

Easy, easy –

Jerry enters the kitchen, stands near Laurel.

LAUREL
(*frozen polite*)

Coffee, Jerry?

JERRY

Oh, no thanks. We bottom-feeders prefer cereal first –

RAY

Let's have Apple Jacks!

DOROTHY
(*in agony*)

Ohhhhhh.

JERRY
(*making her at ease*)

Apple Jacks it is. Dorothy, good morning, darling.

He kisses her on the cheek, in full view of Ray. Dorothy, still embarrassed, not sure what is going on, reaches for cereal.

> RAY

What's going on, Jerry?

> JERRY

A lot. We got a big fax today . . . we need this commission, buddy.

The sisters look at each other. Ray looks around, he feels happy, but there is something else in the room. He shrugs and continues to feel happy.

INT. JERRY'S HOME OFFICE – LATER – DAY

Jerry and Dorothy prepare for the Tidwells.

> DOROTHY

That was great of you this morning.

The Tidwells honk, arriving in the driveway.

> JERRY
> (*friendly, dismissive*)

Look, let's just root for a big offer so we can move out of this room to a real office.

She feels slightly slapped down, but covers. She opens a window quickly, and busies herself with the clutter at hand.

INT. HOME OFFICE – LATER

Fax machine in foreground. The Tidwells have arrived in good spirits, and Rod is telling a story about the first time his father came to a game to watch him play. The story is interrupted by the sound of the fax coming in. Quickly, all four move to the fax.

Everybody has a stake in this fax. Lives are very clearly hanging on these results.

> DOROTHY
> (*to Rod*)

It's going to be great.

Marcee shuts her eyes.

MARCEE

Read it to me, and don't say anything unless it's over nine.

Jerry is the first to read the news. There is a stunning disappointment on the fax.

JERRY

Aw shit –

Rod turns away. Dorothy shuts her eyes, as Marcee opens hers. Tidwell slinks off to sit in a seat too small for him.

MARCEE

One point seven for three years. That's below average. We *owe* more than that . . .

JERRY

I'll go back to them.

MARCEE
(*explodes*)

And say *what*? 'Please remove your dick from my ass!'?
(*a beat*)
I'm sorry. I'm a little pregnant right now.

TIDWELL

I feel like crying. I feel like breaking the room up.

JERRY

Okay, we don't take this emotionally. We *roll* with this problem.

MARCEE

What are you talking about – 'Don't get emotional'. If you ask me, you haven't gotten emotional *enough* about this man. Look at you. I mean, get me Bob Sugar on the phone –

TIDWELL

Honey, don't –

JERRY

You want to leave me?

139

MARCEE
(*to Jerry*)
What *do* you stand for???

Dorothy looks right and left, can't hold back.

DOROTHY
(*furious*)
How about a little piece of integrity in this world that is so
filled with greed and a lack of honorability that I don't know
what to tell my kid except take a look at a guy who isn't
shouting 'Show me the money', he's quietly broke and
working for you for free!
(*off Jerry's pained look*)
Well, I'm sorry, I'm not as good at the insults as she is.

MARCEE
No, that was pretty good.

TIDWELL
(*impressed*)
No shit.

DOROTHY
In fact, you should read something that meant the world to
me . . .

*She opens the drawer, and withdraws the Mission Statement. She is
headed across the room to give it to Marcee, when Jerry swiftly
intercepts it.*

JERRY
Another time, okay, Dorothy?

DOROTHY
Fine, I just –

JERRY
And I appreciate that impulse.

DOROTHY
I think they should see it.

Jerry throws the Mission Statement into a bottom drawer.

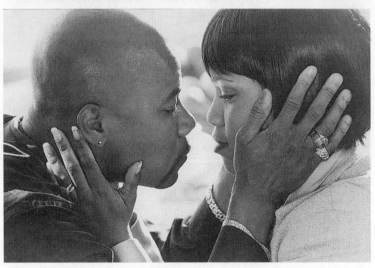

TIDWELL
(*isolated*)
Tell me what to do, Jerry. You tell me to eat lima beans, I'll
eat lima beans. If you say take the shitty deal, that's all we can
get –

MARCEE
'All we can get'?

TIDWELL
Can I *speak* with my agent here?

Marcee is passionate. Focused on Rod.

MARCEE
You know what you're gonna do, Rodney. You're gonna
reject this shitty contract. You're gonna play out your *existing*
shitty contract and go to be a free agent next year and the *hell*
with Arizona. This is us, and *we* determine our worth. You're
a fine, proud, surviving, splendid black man.

TIDWELL
Honey, you are just . . . *the shit.*

*She caresses the back of his neck. He pulls her to him. He gives her a
small kiss. Dorothy and Jerry look at the couple, fascinated and
somewhat uncomfortable. There is a palpable force-field around the
Tidwells.*

JERRY
If you get injured, you get nothing.

TIDWELL
Won't happen. I'm strong in my mind.

JERRY
It's a risk.

TIDWELL
Bet on me, dude. Bet on me like I bet on you.

Tidwell puts his hand out. Maguire is conflicted, but shakes.

EXT. JERRY'S HOME OFFICE — LATE AFTERNOON

Tidwell and Marcee exit. Dorothy and Jerry on the lawn.

> JERRY
>
> I'll get you some quick work —

> TIDWELL
>
> Good deal, man.

> MARCEE
>
> I'm sorry what I said back there.

> JERRY
>
> Don't be silly.

> MARCEE
>
> My husband believes in you. We're gonna make it. Bye bye, Dorothy.

> DOROTHY
>
> Take care, you guys.

Tidwells exit. Finally, Dorothy and Jerry are alone. The Tidwell situation has left an ominous feeling in the air.

> Well, I gotta take that job in San Diego, so don't worry about me. But, Jerry, what you need to do —

> JERRY
>
> Don't even talk about that yet. I'll find something fast for Tidwell. We'll stay afloat.

AIRPLANE WHEELS

touching down.

EXT. COMMERCIAL SET/KAMMELL CHEVROLET/ARIZONA — DAY

Tidwell stands on the set of a regular Arizona car commercial. Three other bored, large Arizona athletes wait by a coffee machine, as Jerry's friend, director Bill Dooler, appears ready to implode. Nearby, a camel.

> TIDWELL
>
> No, dude, *know your art form.*

JERRY

Rod, get on the camel.

DOOLER
(*shoots look to Jerry*)
The sponsor wants a camel –

TIDWELL

Jerry, back me up. It's either the camel or *me* . . .

Tidwell waves his arms, spooking the camel, who spits and stomps.
Several crew members scatter in various directions.

JERRY
(*takes bullet*)
All right. Enough. I'm pulling him out of this. This isn't what
I had in mind anyway.

DOOLER

Then you shouldn't have begged me to hire him.

EXT. SET – LATER

Jerry and Tidwell walk quickly from the set. In the background, another
athlete rides the camel. Jerry rubs face.

TIDWELL

You're learning to be my agent, man! We ain't ever gonna
bring Reebok to their knees doing some regional camel ad.

JERRY

Can I ask you a question totally unrelated to your career?

TIDWELL

Oh, we gonna be friends now?

JERRY

What do you know about dating a single mother?

TIDWELL

Oh I know plenty. I was raised by a single mother.

JERRY

Tell me, because she's about to take another job in San
Diego.

144

TIDWELL

First, single mothers don't 'date'. They have *been to the circus*, you know what I'm saying? They have been to the puppet show and they have *seen the strings*. You love her?

JERRY

How do I know?

TIDWELL

You know when you know. It makes you shiver, it eats at your insides. You know? It's a terrible, terrible thing – You know?

Jerry nods, makes a yes and no gesture.

JERRY

No, I don't know.

TIDWELL

Then you gotta have The Talk.

JERRY

You know, I mean, I'm feeling a little . . . I don't want her to leave. I've been hanging at her place a lot.

TIDWELL

I feel you. I feel you, dog. But you must be fair to her. A single mother, that's a sacred thing, man, gotta have The Talk.
(*beat*)
She loves you, you don't love her. You gotta tell her. Gotta have The Talk.

JERRY

The kid is amazing.

TIDWELL
(*shaking head*)
No. A real man does not shoplift the 'pooty' from a single mom.

JERRY

I didn't 'shoplift the pooty'. We were thrown together and – I mean it's two mutual people who –
(*a look*)

145

All right, I shoplifted the pooty.

TIDWELL
Shame on you. *Shame* on you.

Jerry exits, rubbing face.

EXT. DOROTHY'S FRONT YARD – DAY

A U-Haul is parked in the driveway.

EXT. DOROTHY'S LIVING ROOM – DAY

LAUREL
(*putting her together*)
When you say goodbye, don't make a big dramatic thing out
of it. Be cool. If it's meant to be, it's meant to be. You'll still
see each other. I mean, come on, what about *me*? I'm losing
the only person who really listens to me, and you only listen
to me *partially*.

DOROTHY
Quit making me laugh.

LAUREL
You're doing the right thing. You need to start your life and
he . . . he needs a warm body to cushion the fall. Check out
exhibit A on the front lawn. I'm almost sympathetic to the
guy.

POV - the sisters.

*We see Jerry saying goodbye to Chad too many times. He's anxious not
to be left alone. Finally Chad grabs him by the shoulders, says
goodbye, as a sad Ray trudges to the cab of the U-Haul.*

EXT. DOROTHY'S PLACE – DAY

Jerry scoots a very sad Ray over, and talks to him in the car.

JERRY
I'm not good at this.

Ray begins to cry. Jerry is incapable of dealing with it.

146

I'll see you this weekend, okay?

Ray wails. Jerry squeezes his shoulder, it does nothing, so he exits. He rises and faces Dorothy, keys in hand.

JERRY

Sure you're okay to drive this?

DOROTHY

This rig? Phht. No problem.

JERRY

So I'll see you this weekend.

She accepts it casually, with a shrug.

DOROTHY

All right, so goodbye and – I'll see you in a couple days and –
(*simple, with shrug*)
I love you.

JERRY
(*too quick, weirdly*)
. . . I love you too, you know.

She reacts with an odd look. The words don't sound right, and he knows that she knows.

What –

DOROTHY

Nothing.

JERRY

I'll see you soon.

She turns, decides to say it.

DOROTHY

Look, just in case this weekend becomes next month and next month becomes whatever . . .
(*beat*)
Don't make a joke of your life. Go back and read what you wrote. You're better than the rest of them, better than the Bob Sugars, and don't forget it.

147

She kisses him, and moves quickly toward the car, leaving him alone in frame. He grows increasingly uncomfortable, watching her leave.

> JERRY

Wait a second.

ON DOROTHY

Moving to her car, she hears him. It's not loud enough for her.

Wait a second!

She stops, turns, and he is now close to her.

> JERRY

I know a way to s . . . to save on medical and rent and . . . look . . .

He grips one hand with the other. Dorothy looks at his strange behaviour. He looks over to the cab, where Ray is making a sad face at him through the window.

. . . what if we stayed together? What if we uh . . . got married?

She looks at him. It's an odd proposal.

If I said that, would you stay?

> DOROTHY

No no. Don't do that. Don't say that if you don't . . .
> *(beat)*

Well, say it if you want to.

> JERRY
> *(beat)*

Will you marry me?

She grabs him, and whispers in his ear. Words that speak to his soul.

> DOROTHY

Give me half a chance and I'll make you twice as happy.

She kisses his neck and runs back to the house, to tell Laurel. Jerry moves to Ray.

What's going on?

JERRY

Well, uh, I'm marrying your mother.

He shares the small, emotional moment with Ray, as Dorothy runs off happily, crazily to her sister.

INT. DOROTHY/LAUREL HOUSE – DAY

Laurel watches in horror as her sister comes running back to her.

DOROTHY

Laurel! Guess what . . . !

EXT. DOROTHY'S BACKYARD – DAY

Rod Tidwell sings Marvin Gaye's 'What's Going On' at the wedding for assorted guests here in the backyard, including Marcee and Tyson. Contrary to his own belief, Rod is not a gifted singer. In the wedding band, standing on a small stage in the corner, are Chad and Dooler.

ON JERRY, *who stands watching, smile pasted on, with Father and well-dressed Brother. They are the stoic Maguires.*

BROTHER

Where are all your friends?

JERRY
(*looking around*)

In the band.

INT. DOROTHY'S LIVING ROOM – DUSK

We are CLOSE ON *Ray now as we hear the sound of a Reverend reading wedding vows. Ray holds the ring, and waits for his cue to offer it. And every time the Reverend pauses, he starts to offer the ring. Dorothy's leg and hand are visible in frame. She calms him with a hand on the shoulder. And finally the cue comes and he offers the ring.*

INT. DOROTHY'S HALLWAY/KITCHEN – NIGHT

The bride and groom catch each other, post-wedding, in the hallway.

Wow. We actually –

JERRY

Yeah, we did.

Giddy, Dorothy heads into the living room where friends and relatives watch the video of the wedding. She stands as they watch the coverage of the moment before Dorothy arrives. The camera catches this moment – Jerry turning to Tidwell nearby, shrugging, as if to say, 'What the hell, why not?'

ON DOROTHY

She pauses, pretends not to take it too seriously.

ON JERRY

In the next room.

The enormity is evident on Jerry's face. Much laughter and family noise in the background now. He holds on to a table for a moment, steadies himself. Jerry takes a breath and moves into the kitchen. Finds a beer. He turns and finds himself alone with Laurel, for the first time. She raises her beer. They toast, warily.

LAUREL

If you fuck this up, I'll kill you.

JERRY

(*as she exits*)

Glad we had this talk!

Nearby, Tidwell moves to Jerry. Confidentially:

TIDWELL

You never had 'The Talk', did you?

JERRY

No.

TIDWELL

Well, this was another way to go.

Jerry smiles. Dorothy brings Jerry a Polaroid someone took, and for a moment the couple stand awkwardly together. Tidwell rubs Jerry's shoulders a little, announcing:

This is my agent, man! And we're all gonna have a great season!

He pounds Jerry on the back, hard, shaking him like a pinata.

FADE TO:

SERIES OF SHOTS (FOOTBALL MONTAGE)

Tidwell moves through the season, taking mighty hits. Insert shot of his getting treatment. Now, more hits, leading us to . . .

EXT. PHILADELPHIA PLAYING FIELD – DAY

Tidwell catches the ball, takes a vicious hit.

INT. PHILADELPHIA PRESS BOX – DAY

Jerry moves through the crowded press box, pressing shoulders, working the cause for Tidwell. Across the room, he sees GM Dennis Wilburn standing with Avery. They share a look. He turns away, passing a monitor where elsewhere in the country, Frank Cushman is having another sensational Sunday.

INT. TIDWELL LIVING ROOM/PHOENIX – DAY

This is the Tidwell family ritual of watching Rod's games on the big-screen home TV. At the center is pregnant Marcee Tidwell. Everything flows from her. Next to her is Tyson, and then the cousins, the neighborhood friends. At this particular moment, they are all screaming for Rod, who is taking a beating, but is having a hell of a game. In front of the TV, Tyson does the 'Daddy Dance', a dance of pure joy.

> TYSON
> (*proudly, to family*)
> That's my motherfucker!

Marcee reaches out and collars her dancing son.

> MARCEE
> Why don't you be the first man in your family not to say that word? And then we'll let you live.
> (*as Tyson nods wide-eyed*)
> Now go kiss your daddy, quick.

Tyson dances over to the screen and kisses his dad's graphic image.

> TEE PEE
> That's why they cheer, you know. The white man sending the black man into battle . . .

Marcee shoots him a look, as Tidwell takes another rough hit. The ball squirts out of his hands.

INT. STADIUM HALLWAY – NIGHT

Jerry stands waiting. Bob Sugar nearby, greeting quarterback John Swenson. Still no Tidwell.

INT. LOCKER ROOM – NIGHT

Tidwell sits alone at his locker, as fully dressed Patricia Logan and other media talk to weary naked players other than himself.

EXT. PHILADELPHIA LOCKER ROOM – NIGHT

Finally, here comes Tidwell, moving very slowly with garment bag.

JERRY

How's your head?

TIDWELL

Bubblicious.

He pauses to sign an autograph for a man in a wheelchair. Randall Cunningham passes, pats Tidwell. After a moment, they move on.

The quarterback sucks, man. He's gonna get me killed.

JERRY

I'm a little worried –

TIDWELL

I'm worried too. I'm worried that the only reason I'm here getting my brains blown loose is that you weren't asshole enough to get my ten million three months ago –

INSANE FAN
(*interrupting loudly*)
Fuckin' Rod Tidwell you rule you rule! You rule! I won a fuckin' a fuckin' mug on you in my Rotiss . . . Rotiss . . .

TIDWELL

Peace, my drunken brother. And don't discuss gambling with me.

Expertly, he guides Insane Fan to another player.

JERRY

We can still take the offer, Rod.

TIDWELL

I'm gonna have the game of my life on *Money Night Football*, and show all these motherfuckers.

JERRY

Take care, okay? You're my entire client roster.

TIDWELL

Don't I know. Now go home to your wife.

JERRY

What's that supposed to mean?

155

TIDWELL

Why are you even here, man? You could have told me all this over the phone.

JERRY

I don't know – how's 'dedication' for an answer?

TIDWELL

You don't want to go home, do you?

JERRY

Why are you doing this to me, Rod?

TIDWELL

I'm asking you a question –

JERRY

No, you're –

TIDWELL

I'm trying to talk to you. How's your marriage?

Jerry looks at Rod for a moment. It is the simplest question, and one for which he has no quick answer.

JERRY

Not everyone has what you have.

TIDWELL

Then why'd you get married? I'm asking you as a friend.

JERRY
(*shaking his head*)

You're jabbing at me.

TIDWELL

I'm sorry I asked.

JERRY

No, I'm going to answer you. You want an answer? I'll give it
to you. Loyalty. She was loyal.
(*unconvincing*)

Everything grew from there.

TIDWELL

That's an answer.

JERRY

Damn right.

Tidwell laughs. He doesn't notice that Jerry is truly stung.

Look. I'm happy to entertain you, as always, but I have a
question for you. Are we really 'friends'?

TIDWELL

Why not –

JERRY

Well, friends can tell each other anything, right? If we have
our 'friends' hats on –

TIDWELL
(*wary*)

I think so . . .

JERRY
(*intense*)

Alright. Here's why you don't have your ten million dollars
yet. You are a *paycheck* player. You play with your *head*.

157

Not your heart. In your personal life?
>   (*points*)
Heart. But when you get on the field –
>   (*finger rises to Tidwell's head*)
– you're a businessman. It's wide-angle lenses and who
fucked you over and who owes you for it. That's not what
inspires people. I'm sorry, but that's the truth, can you handle
it? Just a 'question', Rod. Between friends.

Tidwell blinks for a moment.

And when they call you 'shrimp', I'm the one who defends
you.

The word 'shrimp' electrifies Tidwell.

>   TIDWELL
> I don't want to be friends any more.

>   JERRY
> Fine.

>   TIDWELL
> Beautiful.

>   JERRY
>   (*angry*)
> We still getting together in LA?

>   TIDWELL
>   (*angry*)
> Only 'cause my wife likes your wife!

Jerry exits. Tidwell is pissed. And hurt.

'No heart'. 'No heart'?
>   (*yells after him*)
I'm *all* heart, motherfucker!

He gets on the bus.

INT. CRAB RESTAURANT – LATE DAY

*The Tidwells and the Maguires. Tyson and Ray run around the table of
this family-style restaurant. Marcee is very, very pregnant. They crack*

crabs for each other, seasoning for each other, feeding each other like one many-armed and loving body.

> ### MARCEE
> – so I go to see a so-called 'black' film the other day –
> *(then)*
> – honey, no more salt for you, I don't want you dehydrated for *Monday Night Football*. Most important game of your career.
> *(then)*
> – *Twenty* minutes of coming attractions. All black films, all violent, I'm talking about brothers shooting brothers, Wesley Snipes with guns the size of an automobile, blood flowing, cars crashing . . . blood, blood, blood, blood. Is this all they think we want to see? Come on! I enjoyed *Schindler's List*. *Waiting to Exhale* made fifty-nine million at the box office. Doesn't that tell them something? Give me a little credit, I mean, hooo –

> ### TIDWELL
> I hate you going to movies alone without me –

> ### MARCEE
> Oh, baby –

He cracks more crab, gives her the biggest piece.

SHOT OF *Jerry and Dorothy sitting across the table, stunned, just watching this intricate and perfect marriage.*

SHOT OF *Marcee. She takes a breath and gets a weird look.*

> ### TIDWELL
> What, baby?

> ### NICKEE
> Baby. Baby. Baby . . .

INT. DOROTHY'S BEDROOM – NIGHT

Jerry and Dorothy exhausted, alone, getting ready for bed. Dorothy sits down near him on the bed.

DOROTHY

What were you thinking tonight? Watching them go through the complete human emotional experience?

JERRY

I was thinking I hope he doesn't get injured. I felt responsible.

DOROTHY

Sometimes I can't tell at all, what's going through that head of yours.

He makes a noise. As in – it's no big mystery.

And I *really* don't know your noises yet.

Beat of silence.

JERRY

Well, when you wonder, ask me.

DOROTHY
(*unsatisfied*)

Okay . . . I will . . .

Beat. He feels inadequate.

JERRY

Why do you love me?

DOROTHY

Why do you love *me?*

It is, of course, the better question. And before he can answer, there is a pounding at the door.

RAY
(*off-screen*)

Jerry, can I come in and watch TV?

DOROTHY	JERRY
I'll come visit you in a second –	Just for a few minutes, buddy –

The door flies open and Ray comes bounding in, on to the bed, stations himself in the center and begins wrestling Jerry for the remote control.

Dorothy watches, disconnected. A steeliness comes over her that we have not yet seem.

INT. DOROTHY'S KITCHEN – DAY

Dorothy and Laurel in the kitchen.

> LAUREL
> Hang in there, okay? He's not going anywhere.

> DOROTHY
> Yeah . . . I know . . . can we talk about something else?

> LAUREL
> *(beat, dry)*
> I don't think so. I'm incapable of small talk. That's why you love me.

INT. PRESCHOOL – NEXT DAY

Dorothy drops Ray at preschool, and stands in the doorway of the playroom. She watches the boys and girls playing together in a room full of bright colours and games. Music. Anxiety building.

EXT. LOS ANGELES BENCH – NIGHT

Jerry sits on bench, looking.

EXT. RAY'S PLAYHOUSE – DAY

Jerry sits finishing a phone call to an advertising account exec. He has come here, to Ray's playhouse for privacy.

> JERRY
> Tonight. Yeah, and I'll be in Arizona on Monday . . .

Jerry ad libs some salesmanship on Tidwell's behalf. Dorothy approaches. She gives him a few phone messages, sits down. Beat of silence. He sees a look on her face that is unfamiliar.

> DOROTHY
> It's my fault.

JERRY?
What –

DOROTHY
It's not fair to you. This whole –

JERRY
(*instant crisis mode*)
Tell me – let me help –

DOROTHY
I took advantage of you and worst of all, I'm not alone. I did this with a kid. I was just on some ride where I thought I was in love enough for both of us. I pretended that proposal by the car was real . . . It might have been a hypothetical. I did this. And at least I can do something about it now.

JERRY
(*damage control*)
Well – I'm not the guy who's going to run. I stick.

DOROTHY
I don't need you to 'stick'.

JERRY
You want . . .

DOROTHY
I don't know –

JERRY
(*it slips out*)
. . . my soul or something.

DOROTHY
Why fucking not! I deserve it.

JERRY
(*direct*)
Dorothy – what if I'm just not built that way?

DOROTHY
I think we made a mistake here.

But now he can't stop.

JERRY

What if it's true? 'Great at friendship, bad at intimacy.' I
mean, come on. It's the theme of my bachelor film –

DOROTHY

I know. I watched it. I sort of *know it by heart*.

JERRY
(*absorbs it*)

I don't like to give up.

DOROTHY

Oh, please. My need to be the . . .
(*a beat*)
. . . the 'can-do' girl, and your need to be what, 'responsible'
. . . if one of us doesn't say something now we might lose ten
years being polite about it. Why don't we call this next road
trip what it is? A nice long break.

JERRY

What about Ray?

She notes the only real glimpse of ache, in that question.

DOROTHY

There's no question, you'll be friends. Of course you'll be
friends.

JERRY

So this break . . . is a break-up.

DOROTHY

Come on, Jerry. You know this isn't easy for me. I mean, on
the surface, you'd almost think everything was fine. See, I've
got this great guy who loves my kid –
(*resolute, no tears*)
– and *he sure does like me a lot.*

Jerry Maguire, a man who speaks for a living, has nothing to say.

I can't live that way. It's not the way I'm 'built'.

They look at each other. Beat, then:

163

INT. RAY'S ROOM – NIGHT

Jerry kisses sleepy Ray goodbye.

JERRY

Don't wake up . . .

And then faces the exotic fish who now resides on Ray's table. He once lived in a tank the size of a Cadillac. The fish now hangs in a too-small bowl, looking at him.

JERRY
(*defensive*)
. . . it was just a *Mission Statement* . . .

INT. AIRPORT – DAY

Jerry Maguire stretches his arms out. A security wand passes over him. Deadness in his eyes. The glaze of the road on him. Music.

EXT. SUN DEVIL STADIUM/FIELD (ARIZONA) – PRE-GAME
WARMUPS – DUSK

Players from Dallas Cowboys and Arizona Cardinals warm up before
Monday Night Football. *A flash of Frank Gifford on the sidelines,*
Jerry Jones, Tidwell wishing Emmitt Smith a good game.

EXT. SUN DEVIL STADIUM (ARIZONA) – DUSK

We are hovering in the sky, just above Sun Devil Stadium. The classic
Monday Night Football *shot from the blimp.*

INT. MONDAY NIGHT FOOTBALL BOOTH – DUSK

Frank Gifford, Al Michaels, Dan Dierdorf discuss the game.

> GIFFORD
> Now, let's try and untangle this –

> DIERDORF
> If Arizona wins tonight, and next week, and Philadelphia
> loses this Sunday, you can look for the Cardinals to be a
> wildcard entry into the playoffs for the first time in twenty-
> one years. But if Arizona loses and Green Bay wins . . .

INT. TIDWELL LIVING ROOM – NIGHT

Tidwell's family in the living room. A buzz in the air. The pre-game
show is on, sound muted. Old-school on the stereo.

Everybody is happy. Marcee sits in the position of honor, baby Kaydee
in her arms. She is a tired new mother, and the family celebrates her.

> TEE PEE
> He'd better not mess up on *Monday Night Football.*

Marcee shoots Tee Pee a look.

> What did I say? He gets nervous for the TV games . . . It's
> not a secret.

INT. TUNNEL AREA – NIGHT (PRE-GAME)

Nervous Tidwell chews a toothpick as he stands checking out the field.

Nearby, some cheerleaders and a Man in a Pickle Suit.

PICKLE MAN

Nothing like *Monday Night*, huh? What is it, two billion viewers?

TIDWELL
(*irritated*)

Shouldn't you be out there doing some pickle dance or something –?

Pickle Man nods and goes out to dance for the crowd.

VOICE
(*voice-over*)

Hey, Rod – hey, buddydude –

Tidwell turns. It's Bob Sugar approaching. Laser-like, ready to feed on his insecurity.

SUGAR

Listen, I spoke to your quarterback. He's my client, you know. And I said, 'Take care to get those passes down, let Tidwell look good on TV.'

Tidwell looks at him, chews his toothpick.

You should let me do more for you. I would have had you your deal by tonight. Al Michaels is a friend of mine. I would have had him *on the air*, talking about *you*, tonight, when it *counts*.

TIDWELL

Get outta here. Go.

SUGAR

Where's your agent tonight?

TIDWELL

Don't know.

SUGAR

Rod. I know this is 'uncool' to do this now, but you belong with the big boys. You *belong* with the money. You belong with –

Here comes Jerry Maguire.

> **JERRY**
> Get the fuck away from my guy, Sugar.

Tidwell can't help it. He beams as he sees his agent approach.

> **TIDWELL**
> Jerry! You made it –

> **SUGAR**
> Hey, Jerry, hey, buddy. I was just hailing you.

> **JERRY**
> *(prying off Sugar)*
> Go. Flee.

Sugar retreats, offering one final look to Rod.

> **TIDWELL**
> Thanks for coming.

> **JERRY**
> *(bittersweet)*
> I missed ya. What can I say? You're all I've got.

INT. TIDWELL HOME – NIGHT

They watch the game.

> **GIFFORD**
> *(on TV)*
> It's a bruiser out there tonight.

> **MICHAELS**
> *(on TV)*
> Arizona refusing to go into the quiet night of this rough
> football season. Come on, I'm trying to be poetic here.

Tidwell takes a rough hit on the field.

> **DIERDORF**
> *(on TV)*
> Ooof. Another rough hit across the middle on Rod Tidwell.
> Nothing poetic about that.

INT. PRESS BOX – NIGHT

Maguire moves through the crowded box, Avery and Sugar among the crowd in the background.

INT. FIELD – NIGHT

Tidwell takes a hit. Hangs on to the ball.

INT. TIDWELL LIVING ROOM – NIGHT

The Tidwell clan are banging on TV trays and whooping loudly. But in the middle of the cheers, Marcee sees the unsettled look on young Tyson's face. She pulls him over to her, giving him preference over baby Kaydee. He is the only thing in her world.

> MARCEE
>
> What does Daddy say?

> TYSON
>
> 'It looks worse than it is . . .'

Marcee gives him a kiss, as Tidwell makes another grueling gain.

> GIFFORD
> (*voice-over*)
>
> They don't pay enough for a man to take that kind of ugly hit –

> MARCEE
> (*to others*)
>
> Boy, no s-h-i-t.

Big laughs from the living room. Except Tee Pee.

> TEE PEE
>
> He's gonna have nothing left for next season. They're letting him kill himself.

> MARCEE
>
> Can you be quiet?

> TEE PEE
>
> What'd I say?

INT. PRESS BOX – NIGHT

Maguire watches as Arizona's quarterback John Swenson drops back for a pass, and is sacked. Dallas fans cheer wildly. The game is turning uglier by the minute. Jerry looks up to the monitor for a closer look at the next play.

ON PRESS BOX MONITOR: *Swenson, the Arizona quarterback, throws a wobbly pass into the end zone. Tidwell leaps for the catch, tucks the ball in and is promptly and brutally* hit *by two defenders from two different sides. This hit is bad. Worse than bad. Tidwell flips and comes down like a sack of potatoes, with a* thud, *ball still in his hands. His head hits the ground hard. Tidwell is out cold. And the ripple effect of the injury shoots through the stadium. Jerry stares at the monitor, stunned by the sudden brutality.*

EXT. ARIZONA FIELD –NIGHT

We are thrust into the vortex, inside the game. Tidwell lies still on turf. Overhead, the fight music continues for a few seconds before disappearing abruptly. Players and coaches begin to gather around the still body of Rod Tidwell.

INT. TIDWELL LIVING ROOM – CLOSE ON TV – SLOW MOTION

The hit in replay. It is brutal. *And we can see a flash of his pride as he catches the lousy pass, and then . . . like two bulls, the Dallas defenders enter from each side.. One cuts his legs out from under him, and Rod's taut body literally flips. The second defender then hits him at the shoulders. Tidwell lands on the back of his neck, crumpling downwards. Still holding the ball. Still.*

INT. TIDWELL LIVING ROOM – NIGHT

Silence. Utter silence.

> GIFFORD
> (*voice-over*)
> – you sure hope his family wasn't watching that.

And then, in a cry that gurgles from way down deep, Marcee begins to sob. Camera catches the face of Tyson, now panicked. Scared, he embraces his mother.

INT. BOWELS OF SUN DEVIL STADIUM

Maguire sprints through the inner bowels of the stadium. He turns the corner, into the tunnel, talking his way past a guard, heading into the bright TV light of the football field.

INT. TIDWELL LIVING ROOM – NIGHT

Gathering around the television, the family waits through a commercial for more information on Rod's injury.

> TEE PEE
> He should have kept his head tucked down.

> MARCEE
> *(immediately)*

Shut up!!!

> TEE PEE
> I'm not putting him down, I just have a commitment to the truth.

Marcee lunges for him.

> MARCEE
> Can't you be loyal to your brother who *loves* you??
> *(as she is held back)*
> *Get out of my house!*

Across the room, the phone starts ringing. A Cousin answers.

> COUSIN
> It's Jerry Maguire!

Nickee runs to the phone.

INTERCUT WITH:

EXT. ARIZONA FIELD – NIGHT

Jerry Maguire is on the portable.

> JERRY
> He took a shot. He's unconscious.

MARCEE

I'm freakin' out. Oh, God, I'm –

JERRY

Keep the phone open. I'll call back. Stay calm. He's got some good doctors out there.

MARCEE

'Stay calm'? I'm freakin' . . .

JERRY

Alright, I'm freaking, too. But they need you to stay calm. I'll call back.

MARCEE

My whole life is this family, Jerry. It doesn't work without him.

She takes a big gulp, as Jerry watches an overzealous Trainer run out on to the field to join the cluster around the fallen Tidwell. Jerry covers phone and yells on to the field.

JERRY

Don't touch him!!!

EXT. CENTER OF PLAYING FIELD – NIGHT

We're now just a few inches in front *of his peaceful, sleeping face. They are all yelling, trying to pull him out.*

SHOTS OF NATIONAL TELEVISION AUDIENCES

1 A full sports bar in Arizona silently watches Monday Night Football

2 Generic living room of sports fans, all watching Tidwell. Pinned to the screen.

3 Generic outdoor barbecue as fans watch TV.

4 Tidwell living room. All gathered around the television.

5 Maguire straining at the sideline.

6 Monday Night Football *booth. The three announcers watch.*

ON TIDWELL – CLOSE

Dead to the world as sound disappears. There is now only silence.

POV TIDWELL – SLOW MOTION – SILENCE

The Doctors and the Trainers are now truly panicked. We don't hear them. We see them, their motions increasingly manic.

Shoving fingers in front of him. Screaming. We read their lips. ('Rod!' 'Rod, can you hear us?') We see the anguish and escalating fear on their faces. The Trainer leans in close, bellowing, he spreads his hands wide to clap right in front of Rod's still face. His hands head toward each other . . . closer . . . bringing with them the first inkling of sound . . . getting closer and then finally coming together, bringing with him the sounds of the stadium.

ON TIDWELL
Who blinks back to life. Concerned men are yelling very loudly, right in his face. Tidwell becomes aware he is the absolute center of attention of the entire stadium. As crowd noise begins to rise.

> TRAINER
> *Let's get you off the field!*

> TIDWELL
> Wait.

> TRAINER
> *Can you feel your legs?*

> TIDWELL
> Yeah. Just let me enjoy this for a minute.

ON JERRY
Who watches. Only marginally relieved. Is he okay?

ON FANS
Crowd noise rises. Is he okay?

ON TIDWELL
Can he move? Is he okay?

ON TIDWELL'S LIVING ROOM
Not a breath is taken. Is he okay?

ON TIDWELL

He rises. Stadium explodes. At first on wobbly feet, he raises the football and – for the first time – salutes the crowd. Crowd noise doubles.

ON MAGUIRE
gasping for breath.

ON TIDWELL
Has never felt like this before in his life. It is the pure and absolute love of the spotlight. And his fans. And then . . . it's real and he feels it. Tidwell breaks out in a small but unmistakable move – a flutter step. He does a high-stepping move, all his own, for about ten yards.

ON JERRY MAGUIRE
Who watches, now in complete disbelief. Tidwell will not let go of the spotlight.

ON TIDWELL'S LIVING ROOM
Going absolutely nuts. Marcee hysterical, laughing and crying.

>   MARCEE
>   (*to Tee Pee*)
> You ain't talking now, are you??? You're a *silent motherfucker!*

Tyson watches in silent awe of his mother.

BACK ON TIDWELL – CLOSE
Finishes his small but heartfelt dance. He is sharing his personal catharsis now with two billion people. He moves past Jerry Maguire on his way off the field. He looks at Jerry, casually thumps his heart twice.

Jerry Maguire is overcome with emotion. He sits down on a camera case, head in his hands. Behind him, a stadium cheers a new hero.

>   OVERHEARD FAN
> I always knew he was great.

Maguire rubs his face. Overcome. Photographers and others rush past to be closer to Tidwell, who now leaps *into the crowd.*

INT. TUNNEL - LATER

Jerry Maguire surrounded by well-wishers and backslappers. Success has returned, in all its superficial glory. Try as he might, he can't manufacture the joy of the moment. There is a void.

Over the heads of the heatseekers we see Dennis Wilburn nodding, holding a thumbs up. He tries to get to Maguire, but cannot. And then a commotion behind them all.

REPORTER

It's Tidwell!

Tidwell exits the locker room. Press and media surround him. Patricia Logan gives him a look of respect. Even the grizzled old-time stadium workers reach in to squeeze him, to slap him, to touch him. He works his way to Maguire. They hug. Cameras flash. Tears roll down from beneath his purple shades.

TIDWELL

We did it.

ON SUGAR AND SWENSON (*watching them*)
Bob Sugar watches from the nearby wall where he stands with his client, quarterback John Swenson.

SWENSON

Why don't we have that kind of relationship?

BACK TO MAGUIRE AND TIDWELL

And now, in the middle of this emotional union, a portable phone rings. Both men reach for their porties. It's Maguire's. With anticipation, he answers.

JERRY

Dorothy?

Hold on his face for a moment, the disappointment is clear.

It's Marcee. She says she couldn't get through on your phone.

Tidwell grabs the phone, and joyously shares the moment with his wife. Jerry watches, backing against the wall.

TIDWELL

Marcee . . . I'm okay . . . I'm okay . . . nobody's gonna hurt *me.* I got too hard a head!

PUSH IN ON JERRY MAGUIRE
Standing against the wall, just another fan in this crowded hallway, Maguire feels a deep and unexpected loneliness.

175

TIDWELL

How's my baby girl? How's Tyson? I love you so much. You know it isn't real unless I can share it with you –

Jerry turns and heads down the hallway, gaining speed as he walks.

INT. AIRPORT – NIGHT

Jerry Maguire sprints through the empty airport, heading for the flight out of town. Music.

INT. DOROTHY'S LIVING ROOM – NIGHT

The divorced women's group in session.

Laurel stands near the doorway. Camera finds Dorothy, picking up items in the living room, cleaning up a little. She decides to speak her mind.

DOROTHY

I've listened to you all tell a thousand sob stories, and I have been very judgmental. Frankly, I think you've all been *waaaay* too comfortable with your pain. Plus, Jan, you always spill your red wine on the couch.
        (*off Jan's guilty look*)
I've not been fair to you. Women need to stick together, and not depend on the affections of a man to 'fix' their lives. Maybe you're all correct. Men are the enemy.

Murmurs of agreement, some dissent.

But I still love the enemy.

Murmurs of full disappointment.

EXT. DOROTHY'S HOUSE – NIGHT

Jerry exits cab, holding hang-up bag. Looks at the house. On the other side of the window is a world he hopes he's still a part of.

INT. LIVING ROOM – NIGHT

Jerry enters. Dorothy is seated toward the back.

176

JERRY

Hello. I'm looking for my wife.

Dorothy looks up, robbed of words. Stunned, she does not move.

If this is where it has to happen, then this is where it has to happen.
(*off her silence*)
I'm not letting you get rid of me. How about that?

He shares a look with some of the other women. She's not going to say a word. Neither do they.

This used to be my specialty. I was good in a living room. Send me in there, I'll do it *alone*. And now I just . . . I don't know . . . but tonight, our little project, our 'company' had a very big night. And it wasn't complete, wasn't nearly close to being in the same *vicinity* as complete, because I couldn't share it with you. I couldn't hear your voice, or laugh about it with you. I missed my wife. We live in a cynical world, and we work in a business of tough competitors, so try not to laugh –
(*directly*)
I love you. You complete me.

177

DOROTHY

Aw, shut up. You had me at hello.

He moves to her. They embrace. Ray watches in background. Jerry has given this room hope. It's on their faces. At last, even Laurel signs off on her sister's happiness. She shares a look with Chad, who knows he has lost the secret love of his life. The warm and silent moment washes over all of them. And then:

WOMAN #1

This is one of the better talk groups I've been to.

JAN
(*sloshing wine*)

I think we'd better go . . .

INT. ROY FIRESTONE SHOW – NIGHT

FIRESTONE

. . . your father who left the family on Christmas Eve, the mother who cleaned the steps of a prison to make your tuition. The older brother who lost a leg in that tragic bass fishing accident –

Tidwell is wearing glasses now, in a somewhat scholarly mode.

TIDWELL

No, Roy. I'm not gonna cry.

Smiling, Firestone looks down at the card in his hand.

FIRESTONE

– Well, Rod, your agent passed me a note before the show. He says that your deal memo has been signed by the Arizona Cardinals. Four years for ten point two million dollars. Playing in the state where you grew up.

ON TIDWELL – *weeping*

I . . . I love everybody, man. I love my wife. My kids. Little Tyson. My new baby Kaydee. My brother Tee Pee. I love my friends, my team mates, who am I leaving out?

178

FIRESTONE
(*laughing*)
It's only a half-hour show, Rod.

ON TIDWELL'S FRIENDS AND FAMILY

Marcee crying, too. Shot takes us to Jerry, Dorothy and Ray.

TIDWELL
Wanna send some beautiful love out to my offensive line, just
a beautiful bunch of dudes, wanna thank a beautiful
individual – God, and of course the entire Arizona
organization, a little slow, but they do come around. I'm
leaving somebody out . . .

*Amused and finally glimpsing the end of a long journey, Jerry leans
over to Marcee.*

JERRY
Take care, Marcee. We'll see you at the restaurant.

She nods, emotionally, biting her lip.

TIDWELL
Oh, yes! Jerry Maguire! My agent! This is a fierce, loving
individual, I love this man, he *is* love, he is *about* love – my
ambassador of kwan.

FIRESTONE
Ten seconds, Rod.

TIDWELL
And I love my fans, of which he is one. Wanna thank them
for all my Sundays, and of course my Monday nights, too.
That about says it. . .

*Jerry watches the monitor wondrously before leaving. TV credits are
rolling on the show.*

Wait! and thank you, Melvin from the Casual Man, thank you
for the suit.

EXT. PARKING LOT – DAY

Jerry, Dorothy, Ray exit into the daylight. They walk to Jerry's car.

179

From across the fence, a stray baseball from a pickup game flies into the parking lot and bounces ahead of them. Ray picks it up. In an easy fluid motion, he whips it back over the fence to the game on the other side. A few kids on the other side of the fence shout their approval of a great little throw.

Jerry and Dorothy stop, looking at Ray, who has just shown shocking natural ability. They are quiet for a moment, then turn slowly to look at each other. And then, not ready to deal with it, not even close to ready to deal with it, they say quickly to the boy:

JERRY	DOROTHY
Come on, Ray.	Ray, let's go.

Happily, Ray joins them as they walk to the car. A family.

FADE OUT.

TIDWELL COMMERCIAL REEL – WITH END CREDITS

FADE IN:

Rod in a beautifully composed head-shot, talking to us. Already we know this – he is not the world's best actor. But he is so at home, so happy at the sheer prospect of making this commercial, that he shines.

> TIDWELL
> There are several things I will not do.

INT. CONCERT STAGE – NIGHT

Rod Tidwell stands in a glittery suit, singing a Luther Vandross-style ballad. In the audience, several people wince.

EXT. ICE RINK – DAY

Tidwell on skates, skating. The ice breaks.

INT. SHOPPING MALL – NIGHT

Tidwell in big sweater, hawking an Icesickle. It's melting.

ON TIDWELL – *shaking his head.*

> TIDWELL

No.

ON TIDWELL – PROFILE.

There are things I *should* not do.

INT. BARBER SHOP – DAY

Tidwell has given himself pink Rodman-style hair. He digs himself. The barber knows better. Holds up a mirror.

INT. SEVEN-ELEVEN – NIGHT

Tidwell buys sanitary napkins at the counter of a Seven-Eleven. Two other guys in line exchange looks.

CLOSE SHOT *of Tidwell shaking his head.*

> TIDWELL

No.

ANOTHER ANGLE

But there is one thing I know how to do –

SERIES OF SHOTS

All the shots of Tidwell we've seen, making his brutal catches, passing through bone-crushing blocks.

ON A SHOT OF EVER-READY BATTERY
which turns out to be a wall, which Tidwell comes crashing through.

> TIDWELL

Survive.

A moment after his defiant look, he cracks up and it's a perfect flub.

SHOT OF *him laughing. Posing for a picture with the crew. On the very outskirts, Jerry Maguire. For Rod Tidwell, it's like a graduation shot. And it ends his first commercial.*

ON BLACK.

FADE IN *the sound of applause.*

These words appear: Rod Tidwell

Then these words appear: We ignored him for years.

Then these words appear: We were wrong.

Then these words appear: We're sorry.

Then these words appear: Reebok.

THE THINGS WE THINK AND DO NOT SAY
Thoughts of a Sports Attorney

It's I a.m. and this might be the bad pizza I had earlier talking, but I believe I have something to say. Or rather, I have something to say that I believe in. My father once said, 'Get the bad news over with first. *You* be the one to say the tough stuff.' Well, here goes. There is a cruel wind blowing through our business. We all feel it, and if we don't, perhaps we've forgotten how to feel. But here is the truth. We are less ourselves than we were when we started this organization.

Sports Management International began as a small company. I was hired by Jack Scully in 1981, I was fresh out of college, I didn't even *watch* much sports. But a young man came to me, and his name was Bill Apodaca. He asked me to look at a contract he'd acquired to play football for the Atlanta Falcons. Before long I was overseeing the business of another member of the Falcons, and two baseball players. The nuances and the small miracles of professional sports would soon hook me – there was something simple and perfect about the way a stadium *felt*. The way *you* felt when a player you'd helped and represented made his stand in front of 54,000 people. And I remember the conversation Mr Scully and I had by an elevator, standing next to one of those sand-filled ashtray posts, right before he hired me as one of the first agents in this company. 'You and I are blessed,' he said, 'we do something that we love.'

Tonight, I find those words guiding me back to an important place, and an important truth. I care very much about the fact that I have learned to care less. Now our company is one of the top three in this business, and we represent over a thousand athletes. Over sixty agents work at our huge new office, and I still haven't met all of you. The business of sports has never been bigger, or tougher, or more written about. And we are at the forefront. But I wonder tonight, as we leave our thirteenth annual conference . . . We've talked a lot and partied a lot over the last three days, but I dare say that not one of us, our diet Pepsis and sheaf of papers in hand, have said what we really think.

It is beyond the easy arguments waged against sports, and our business on the editorial pages of the *New York Times*. It is beyond the huge salaries, the endorsements all our clients now want because 'I'm a better actor than Michael Jordan.' Beyond the globalization and merchandization of the games. It's more subtle than the baseball strike, more about loyalty than the Colts moving to Indiana, the Rams going to St Louis, or the Cleveland Browns moving to . . . someplace. I'm talking about something they don't write about. I'm talking about something we don't talk about.

We are losing our battle with all that is personal and real about our business. Every day I can look at a list of phone calls only partially returned. Driving home, I think of what was not accomplished, instead of what *was* accomplished. The gnawing feeling continues. That families are sitting waiting for a call from us, waiting to hear the word on a contract, or a general manager's thoughts on an upcoming season. We are pushing numbers around, doing our best, but is there any real satisfaction in success without pride? Is there any real satisfaction in a success that exists only when we push the messiness of real human contact from our lives and minds? When we learn not to care enough about the very guy we promised the world to, just to get him to sign. Or to let it bother us that a hockey player's son is worried about his dad getting that fifth concussion.

There is a good bet that I will erase all of this from my laptop, and you will never read it. But if you are reading it, and you're reading it right now, it is only because I was unable to stop. I was unable to forget the quiet questions in the hallways, when some of you, usually the younger agents, or interns, asked me on the side: 'How do you keep all these lives, all these clients, separated in your mind?'

Chances are, I didn't say much. I might have told you 'It's easy' or 'You're not working hard enough.' Chances are, I said something that you expected, maybe even wanted to hear. But it wasn't the truth, and it wasn't what I felt. And if you ever wondered about the drawbacks of being quiet about important things, talk to yourself in the mirror some time, say the truth. Yell

184

the truth to yourself, when no one is listening. See how good it feels?

My father worked for the United Way for thirty-eight years. We lived in San Diego for many years before I left to move up the coast to Los Angeles. One of the things my father said was: 'Every time you allow a problem in your life, you are actually at a point of transformation. Crisis is a powerful point of transformation.' (Never mind that he sat in the same chair for thirty-eight years, and when he retired said only that he wished he'd asked for a more comfortable place to sit.)

We are now at a point of transformation with this company. But this is not something to fear, it is something to celebrate. Because I come to you tonight, looking out at the dark Miami skyline, not only with a challenge. I come to you with answers too.

But first let us define our position.

Right now we are at breaking point with our client list. We are not so huge that we must hire more agents, and not so small that we have not experienced huge success. We are at a point of neutrality. We are all, right now, neutral. Neutral, as in not black or white. Not bad or good. Even. Neutral.

Even in my own life, after thirty-five years, I feel that I have never done that one thing, that noble thing that defines a life. Even writing this Mission Statement is odd for me. I am used to flying below the radar, enjoying my life and friends. But I have not been truly tested. I have not gone to India to explore my life, as my brother has. I have not been in a major car accident, or fathered a child. I have not created a life, nor have I killed anyone. I am neutral. I haven't started a war, and I haven't stopped a war. I have broken even with my life. I have nice home, a nice car, a fiancée who makes my heart race. But I have not taken that step, or risk, that makes the air I have breathed for thirty-five years worthwhile. I once had a yellow couch. I got rid of it because it was neutral. My life is now like that yellow couch.

And yet, as I sit here in the wonderful Miami Hilton, I have never been so happy to be alive. I have said 'later' to most anything that required true sacrifice. *Later* I will spend a weekend reading real books, not just magazines. Later I will visit my grandmother who is a hundred and unable to really know the difference. Later I will visit the clients whose careers are over, but

185

of course I promised to stay in touch. Later later later later. It is too easy to say 'later' because we all believe our work to be too important to stop, minute to minute, for something that might interfere with the restless and relentless pursuit of forward motion. Of greater success. Make no mistake, I am a huge fan of success. But tonight, I propose a better kind of success. I could be wrong, but if you keep reading and I keep writing, we might get there together.

RANDOM FACT # 128:

Sports Management International, founded in 1981, was dedicated to the then rock-solid notion that athletes deserve a decent home with decent pay. The original client roster consisted of four athletes, one of them was the first American Frisbee Champion, Chester Savage, who was actually born in Australia

Now of course we all know that we possess the job of the decade. Last year, when a poll of college students was taken, our occupation, Sports Agent or Sports Attorney ranked number two to Rock Star. But rock stars, like sports stars, have a limited time in the spotlight. Nobody likes an old lineman or a bald rock star. But sports representation can give you a career into your eighties, like the original sports agent Dicky Fox, who died on his way to a Chicago Bulls playoff game in 1993. He died gloriously, right by the B gates, a happy man who had actually written a book called *A Happy Life*. Taken by a heart attack, he left a loving wife and family, and a home next door to his first client. And we won't talk about the two guys who stole his playoff tickets, right out of his pocket as he lay on the cool floor of the O'Hare airport. They were yanked from Dicky's seats in the first quarter, and two guards kept the seats empty in tribute to him.
A Happy Life.
And to those young agents who never met him, Dicky Fox always said the same thing when asked for his secret. 'The secret to this job,' he said, 'is personal relationships.'
We are agents. To some, that brings with it the image of a slickster. A huckster. Someone profiting off the efforts of others. For many of those we've met or observed, that is *exactly* what we

186

are. I know an agent operating in this very state who regularly gets the phone numbers of college athletes by calling school offices and posing as a tutor who has lost their student's contact number. He is often successful in acquiring athletes, but none for very long. Privately, an agent can be a father, a friend, an inspiring force in the life of a young man or woman. We are sometimes as important as priests or poets, but until we dedicate ourselves to worthier goals than getting an illegal phone number, we are poets of emptiness.

Somehow all this has been bubbling up inside me. A man is the sum total of his experiences. And it is now that I am interested in shaping the experiences to come. What is the future of what we do? Give me a goal, and I will achieve it. That has been my secret design for most of my life. Perhaps you are the same. We're all goal-oriented, so I hereby present a goal.

How can we do something surprising and memorable with our lives? How can we turn this job, in small but important ways, into a better representation of ourselves? Most of us would easily say that we *are* our jobs. That's obvious from the late hours we all keep. So then, it is bigger than work, isn't it? It is about *us*.

How do we wish to define our lives? So that when we are sixty, or seventy, or eighty and we're sinking down on to that cool floor of O'Hare airport, with playoff tickets in our pockets, perhaps we too can know that we led *A Happy Life*? Is it important to be a Person and not just a slave to the commerce of Professional Sport? Do we want to be Remembered?

Or do we just want to be the guy who sold the guy who sold shoes that came with the little pump?

Recently I was asked by the son of a client, in so many words, 'What do you stand for?' I was lost for an answer. At fourteen, I wasn't lost for that answer. At eighteen, I wasn't lost for an answer. At thirty-five, I was blown away that I had no answer. I could only look at the face of a twelve-year-old boy, concerned about his dad, needing my help, just looking at me for the answer I didn't have.

The look on that kid's face is a part of me now. And the feeling I had, and have now, is pushing me forward, writing this Mission Statement.

What am I doing? I must erase this entire document. I'll write a little more, save it and go to bed.

My dad was one of the good guys. He studied at West Point, went to Korea in the conflict there. Later, he left a glittering life in the military to move to California, because my mother did not take well to the army life. My father never complained about it. He was prone to tell his war stories, but never in a beery 'you gotta listen to me' way. He was graceful and he was funny, and he didn't complain. For the late part of the sixties and the early seventies, even while doing volunteer work for United Way, as I previously described, he was an operator of Telephone Answering Services. He had two of these businesses. Long rooms filled with telephone operators who cooly answered your phone for you when you were away from home.

'Can I take a message?'

Almost as soon as he began this business, the first automatic telephone answering-machine was introduced on to the market. Our conversations at the table were often about the future, and whether the world would accept these new machines.

'I just can't talk to one,' said my mother.

'Neither can I,' said my older brother. 'Nobody wants to talk to a machine.'

'They'll never last,' said my dad. 'People only like to talk to people.'

Within three years, mechanical answering-machines were everywhere. The whole idea of a human answering your phone while you were away was no longer important. People were talking with machines, regularly and familiarly. Making funny phone messages, personalizing the machine of forward motion that had arrived in their homes. There was no way back. The machine was a part of life, but only when everyone learned to personalize it.

The same thing is true of sports. Sports may never be the pure and simple thing that older men pine for. That ball park in the corn fields of *Field of Dreams* is, of course, a fantasy that lives in the mind. Sports is a huge operation, always was, but now that fact is no longer a secret that lives in the luxury boxes of ownership.

The secret is out of the bag. Way, way out. Everyone knows that Sports is a machine. The Endorsement is now in danger of overshadowing the game. The commercials are often more interesting than the telecast. Money sits on the bench, right alongside the players. The players know, the owners always knew, the fans know. The machine has moved into our homes.

The question is, how do we personalize that machine? It is a question we must now ask ourselves at SMI.

I propose that, like the world embraced those telephone answering devices, we talk to the machines. We deal with the future that is already here. It isn't even the future, it is now, so let us talk to the Machine and see what it says to us.

Let's bring soul and character to what is already there.

I propose that we re-create everything that we're currently about. Right now we're at the top of our game. Traditionally people do one thing at this point in their success. They try like hell to maintain what they did to get there. Their personal and intense road to success, their original inspiration (which is at the heart of every success) is now lost in the pursuit to keep the money machine smoothly rolling forward. Delivering crisp green sheets of greater and greater amounts of fortune. But there is a problem with this stage in the success game. In doing this 'maintain success' cycle, they forget the original glimmer of passion that got them there.

And historically, no one successful ever pauses to think that they might tumble like everyone before them who forgot. The whole success cycle dooms the very thing that causes the success in the first place – it puts shutters on the windows of reality. It makes us all forget that monetary success comes from something very pure. It comes from a desire to do well, to make life better, not just to do well with financial regularity.

Recent telephone conversation with a client who had been accused of 'selling out' by a local columnist:

'Of course I sold out. My only problem is, I sold out *before there was any money in it.*'

It is not easy to hide a winning formula. Take a successful TV show. The following season, you see twenty others just like it.

Same goes for our company. Sports Management International was one of the first great success stories of our business. But the great ones all do one thing at the time of their greatest success. They change the game. They make it harder for themselves. They raise the bar. They work not just harder, but they work smarter. That is why the great athletes, politicians, musicians, philosophers all got stronger instead of more weary. We must do the same. And for those wondering when I will propose an answer to these many questions, I must ask you simply to hold on. Because it's coming.

I have just poured a pot of coffee. Maybe I'm crazy, maybe it's just tonight, but I really do think I'm on to something here. And, as I said earlier, if you're reading this, it means that I didn't conquer this statement with my own fears of rejection. If you knew me, and many of you do, you know that 'rejection' and 'fear' are not words I say easily. But this is more than a Mission Statement. This is not the equivalent of one of those magnetic 'poetry kits', you know, the ones you buy at a stationery store, a mess of words so you can assemble funny poems on your refrigerator door. This is from my heart. This is a love letter to a business I truly love.

MIAMI, 2.37 A.M., THOUGHTS:

Coffee tastes different at night. It tastes like college.

I'm back. Just checked the messages at home, and sure enough one of them was a man I will call Client X. Client X was watching ESPN and he saw Athlete Y talking about the many many millions he has in contracts both in football, baseball and product representation. We have all been on the receiving end of a message like the one I just picked up on my answering-machine.

'Why aren't I making what Athlete Y makes?' said my client. And the truth is obvious to everyone but Client X. Athlete Y is a superstar, and is more talented. But to tell this to Client X would be asking him to become Ex-Client X.

And so begins the game of flattery, of lip service, of doing everything possible to soothe and stroke. It is part of our lives, and part of our jobs. The game of agenting. The tap-dance. Not only will Client X be a tap-dance, but there will be a tap-dance involved in explaining why I didn't return the call and begin the tap-dance earlier. I know it is a tap-dance, and so does he. I have seventy-two clients, and over sixty of them are full-time tap-dances. I sign ten or twelve new ones a year. As many of you know, it is going in the wrong direction.

But as I sit here in the darkness of this hotel room, the answer to the future is rather obvious. If the tap-dancing becomes less constant, less furious, less *necessary*, what will the result be? The result will be more honesty, more focus, fewer clients, but eventually the revenues will be the same. Because the new day of honesty will create a machine more personalized, more truthful, and the client that wasn't bullshitted this year, has a greater chance of greatness next year.

And now we get to the answer that Dicky Fox knew years ago. The answer is fewer clients. Less dancing. More truth. We must crack open the tightly clenched fist of commerce and give a little back for the greater good. Eventually revenues will be the same, and that goodness will be infectious. We will have taken our number oneness and turned it into something greater. And eventually smaller will become bigger, in every way, and especially in our hearts.

Forget the dance.

Focus.

Learn who these people are. That is the stuff of your relationship. That is what will matter. It is inevitable, at our current size, to keep many athletes from leaving *anyway*. People always respond best to personal attention, it is the simplest and easiest truth to forget.

Love the job. Be the job.

The phone calls will still come in at 2 a.m., but on the other end of that phone at 2 a.m. will be someone deserving of your time, and you will be honored to share their time. And that will be what the road to greatness feels like. A little rocky at first. But think how good it will feel to wake up in the morning and know that when the phone rings, it is not Client X demanding the tap-dance. It will be Client K, whose life we know and share in.

Let us be honest with ourselves.

Let us be honest with them.

Forget the dance.

Focus.

I propose this as the very heart of the Mission Statement that is flying across my screen. I am not a writer but I can't stop from writing this. It is something pure, from the deepest part of me. It has to be right, and as one of the Senior Agents at this company, I ask to be heard. And if I am wrong, then grab me by the collar and tell me why you disagree. And I will happily talk with you because we are talking about something that matters.

Down below on the promenade, I see a young girl skating in the night. The simple beauty with which she cascades across the smooth cement, the intelligence with which she uses this path that is crowded with shoppers and businessmen in the daytime. At night, it is hers. She owns it. I feel the same pride of ownership, owning this world that allows me to type this message to you. And perhaps save the future of this company. It is a great feeling, not just that wretched desire to survive, to outswim the huge wave that may drill me into the sand below the water, but to seize this time. To set the agenda. To say what I feel.

MIAMI, 3.13 A.M., THOUGHTS:

I have the distinct feeling that what I have written is 'touchy feely'. I don't care. I have lost the ability to bullshit.

I feel so good about not erasing this Mission Statement. There is so little that we are able to create in this business. Most of the time, we are creating nothing. We are shoving digits around. But to address the growing pains of our business, and to create a new way of looking at what we do . . . because these growing pains could easily be dying pains. But we are meant to live at this company. Our work actually does have an effect on people. In a cynical world, we make people happy. We let them know that one athlete can make a difference.

The same can be said of one company.

RANDOM TRAVEL TIP # 434:

When using a hang-up bag, whenever possible, pack clothes in dry cleaning bags. The extra layer prevents wrinkling.

I propose also that we step up our concerns to build in non-profit areas of our contracts. It is something that we often talk about, sitting in those athletes' living rooms, but often we let these factors slip away. How often have we advised clients to move to Florida, this very state, where taxes are lenient? Let us use the same sharp thinking not just to set up charity golf tournaments, but to help build schools in the communities where many of our finest athletes first found the inspiration to help them on to greatness.

It is important to tweak the greater concerns of our athletes as well. Because the ability to forget social causes happens easily, in the night. Suddenly the desire to survive obscures the quest to give back to a community. If we don't exercise the muscle of charity, one day it is dead. It doesn't respond, it's just a fiber in your body that serves no purpose. And the next thing that happens is the lack of depth that comes with financial prosperity. How many rich people have said this in our presence: 'I thought I would feel better when I was rich, but I don't.'

That happens when we don't listen to the loud sound of the quiet voice inside. Life, I believe, is not a country club where we forget the difficulties and anxieties. Life is the duty of confronting all of that within ourselves. I am the most successful male in my family, but I am hardly the happiest. My brother works for Nasa, helping grow blue-green algae that will one day feed the world. He was originally targeted as the 'successful' one in my family. But he gave up early, for a quieter kind of success. He was once tortured, now he is quietly making the world a better place. He learned earlier what I am just now starting to wake up to. He sleeps well at night. And he doesn't worry about being too preoccupied or too busy to get the dance right. He dances for something greater.

3.32 A.M., MIAMI, THOUGHTS:

Next door, someone named David is having sex. I know because his girlfriend or wife just yelled something out in the throes of ecstasy: 'Put the top back on, David!' I pause and wonder. What did David open, and why does he now have to close it?

You can e-mail the President, you can get sushi in a supermarket in the middle of the desert, you don't even have to read a book anymore – you can buy a tape where it is read out loud. But where is the simple truth about how to live a quality life? I hope that I have not overstepped my boundaries by writing this to you. This is an attempt to reach out, and say loudly the things that have been festering within. And once you begin to speak these things, it's hard to stop.

I have decided to tell you about Mimee. A few days ago I got a phone call from a friend. Mimee Benadetta had died. I barely knew her, she was the girlfriend of a friend. They broke up in the mid-eighties, but Mimee and I had the attraction of two people who might have been together, had circumstances been different. We lost touch. And now she is gone, dead from a car accident, and I find myself thinking about what I could have done while she lived.

Last Christmas I felt the tingle of a thought – call her. I delayed calling, now it is too late. I think that tingle, the small voice inside, is always the voice of what is right. And how much sound and fury exists in our life determines how easy it is to listen.

I miss you, Mimee. You and I both know. We had something that was never followed up on. I wish you well on your journey.

RANDOM AIRPORT FACT # 23:

Denver International Airport is a converted cornfield that sinks $\frac{3}{4}$ inch deeper into mud every year. This airport also contains the best gift-shop, with adjacent ATM access, in the United States.

I have never been a writer, but I can see how this great lost art will never truly die. Putting words to paper is a sacred thing. It's more than a phone conversation, it is a document. It is something you are putting on paper. The relationship between a phone call and a letter is the difference between a magazine and a book. One you leave on a plane, the other you save.

I am too excited to sleep. I want this Mission Statement to last to the light of day. Outside, a passing car plays a snatch of an old Pink Floyd album: 'Money . . . '

I am wondering what that exact moment is when we truly, truly love our jobs. Is it during the day, or at the end of the day, or is it years later looking back on all we accomplished? I think perhaps truly loving something is the ability to love it *at that moment*. It is an elusive ability, something I have never been able to quite accomplish. I must go home, and take my experiences like a squirrel, and consider them, before I can truly enjoy them. I must work on this. The daily journey is everything. Being able to enjoy enjoyment while it is happening. I might erase this part.

4.45 A.M. MIAMI, THOUGHTS:

Whatever David opened, the top is now back on and not much has changed. Does sex really sound this silly? And if it does, why don't people laugh more when they're having it?

Why do I feel more alive for having written all of this? Some of you are younger than me, some of you are older than me. Right now I have one foot in each of your worlds. I am thinking about marriage, and the future, but I'm old enough to have a past that I (hopefully) have learned from. In another hour or so, a *USA Today* will plop at the door, phone calls will come in, and provide a whole new set of distractions to keep me from the central issue, the issue that we have discussed all this week, in various ways and in various forums, but have we really discussed it?

I have now written far too much on the subject of our future, the future of this business. But the beauty of this proposal, I think, is that it is only a slight adjustment, an adjustment in our minds. An adjustment in attitude. An adjustment to a point where we can discuss the things that really matter to us, and our many clients. This coming holiday season, that time when we all know we must work harder to let our clients know what we're doing for them, that difficult time when big decisions are made and agents are often fired, let us really reach out. Let us celebrate the clients that have meant more to us because of this small adjustment.

Let us work less hard to sign the clients that we know won't matter in the long run, and work twice as hard to keep the ones who will. I believe in these words, and while they may not yet be true for you, they are true for me. And I ask that you read this with that in mind. I am dictating not what I want us to be, but what I wish us to be. There is a difference. You can only get there if I have written this correctly, and if you are inspired. I am reaching out to you, personally. I choose to be passionate again. I choose to reclaim everything that was once exciting about this job. I wonder if this might just be the best idea I've ever had. I hope you understand. In the words of Martin Luther King, whose suit I suggest you all visit before they move it from its display in the Atlanta airport: 'A life is not worth living until you have something to die for.'

A life is not worth living if you are sleepwalking through it. Because that is what feels like death. That is what causes athletes to, out of despair, get drunk and wrap their cars around a pole. Or lash out at someone they love. Or that is what might have caused Mimee to career into another car in an oncoming lane of traffic. It is the feeling of sleepwalking. Of others living life around you, keeping their fists tightly wound around whatever dollars they can muster, caring little more than nothing about those around you. We cannot sleepwalk. We cannot just survive, anything goes. We can take control of our lives, we can quit sleepwalking, we can say – right now, these are our lives, it is time to start living it. It is time to not second guess, to move forward, to make mistakes if we have to, but to do it with a greater good in mind.

Let us start a revolution. Let us start a revolution that is not just about basketball shoes, or official licensed merchandise. I am prepared to die for something. I am prepared to live for our cause. The cause is caring about each other. The secret to this job is personal relationships.

PRODUCTION MATERIALS

Here are some artefacts from the filming.

This is our breakneck schedule to release the film by Christmas.
Conspicuously absent from the time-line – sleep.

Start Shooting	11 March '96
Finish Shooting	5 July '96
Editor's Cut	12 July '96
Director's Cut	24 September '96
Screen for TriStar	24 September '96
Director's 1st Preview	26 September '96
Preview Changes	27 September–7 October '96
Director's 2nd Preview	8 October '96
Lock Picture	9 October '96
Turn over to Music & Effects	10 October '96
Start Negative Cutting	28 October '96
Start Timing	30 October '96
Score	28 October–1 November '96
Start Dubbing	31 October '96
Finish Dubbing	20 November '96
Answer Print	26 November '96
Release Date	13 December '96

Shown

I can hear you Rod
I'm still here
You're gonna star w/ me
　　　　　that's great -
　　　I'm very happy
Yes
I'm ready　　　　　　　　　— you ready
I'm ready　　　　　　　　— you ready?
　　　　　　　　　　　　　—
I got it Rod　　　　　　　— show me the money
Show you the $　　　　　— show me the mon
　"　"　"　"　　　　　　—yell it
What's that?
Yell it?　　　　　　　　— No show you, show
Show you the $　　　　　　　me the $
yell Show you the $　　　　　louder
　"　"　"　"
　　"　"　　"　"　　　　　louder
Show Me the $
　　"　"　"　"
　　"　"　"　"
　　"　"　"　"
soft Show me the $
whisper　"　"　"　"
soft Show me the $
soft　"　"　"　"

The 'Show Me The Money' scene grew longer and more riotous
in rehearsals. The verbal jam sessions continued into filming.
Here is the first diagram of the sequence, made for the actors
while we were shooting.

Well Show me the $ ugh

"   "   "   "   This is good
                             you know

"   "   "   "   I love you black men
                             Do you love your
                             black man?

I love you Black man!
    Show me the $!   Do you love black
                             people

I love Black people!   This is good
    Show me the $!

...you're my motherfucker.   you're my
                             motherfucker

"   "   "   "

I'm gonna do it 4 you!   who you gonna
    Mance, I'm   do it for?

I'm gonna Show you the $ what are you
                             gonna do?
"   "   "   "

199

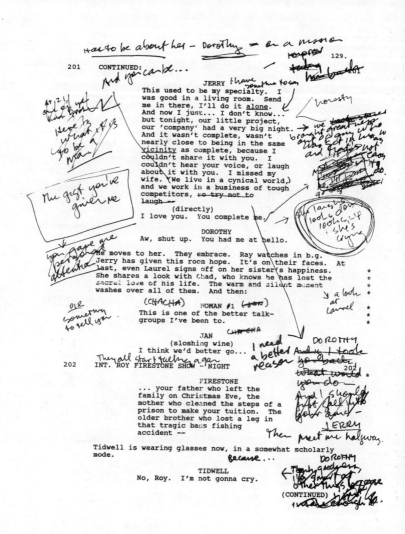

201 CONTINUED: 129.

JERRY
This used to be my specialty. I
was good in a living room. Send
me in there, I'll do it alone.
And now I just... I don't know...
but tonight, our little project,
our 'company' had a very big night.
And it wasn't complete, wasn't
nearly close to being in the same
vicinity as complete, because I
couldn't share it with you. I
couldn't hear your voice, or laugh
about it with you. I missed my
wife. (We live in a cynical world,)
and we work in a business of tough
competitors, so try not to
laugh —
(directly)
I love you. You complete me.

DOROTHY
Aw, shut up. You had me at hello.

He moves to her. They embrace. Ray watches in b.g.
Jerry has given this room hope. It's on their faces. At
last, even Laurel signs off on her sister's happiness.
She shares a look with Chad, who knows he has lost the
secret love of his life. The warm and silent moment
washes over all of them. And then:

(CHACHA) WOMAN #1 (JAN)
This is one of the better talk-
groups I've been to.

JAN
(sloshing wine)
I think we'd better go...

202 INT. ROY FIRESTONE SHOW - NIGHT 202

FIRESTONE
... your father who left the
family on Christmas Eve, the
mother who cleaned the steps of a
prison to make your tuition. The
older brother who lost a leg in
that tragic bass fishing
accident —

Tidwell is wearing glasses now, in a somewhat scholarly
mode.

TIDWELL
No, Roy. I'm not gonna cry.

(CONTINUED)

I was worried about this scene.

200